HOW TO BE HAPPY

HOW TO BE HAPPY

Turning Tiny Steps Into Giant Strides

Pam & Peter Keevil

Peverel Press

Peverel Press

www.peverelpress.com

ISBN (paperback): 978-1-8384674-0-1
ISBN (ebook): 978-1-8384674-1-8

To all those people who've been so generous with their kindness and teachings over the years.

CONTENTS

INTRODUCTION

In 2020, we co-authored a book called *Finding Happiness After Covid-19*. It brought together a wealth of tools and techniques which we have used in our professional and personal lives for many years. We wrote the book during the first lockdown in the UK and did not foresee the long period of time this pandemic would affect the lives of so many millions of people. The Covid-19 pandemic has severely tested many people's sense of happiness and wellbeing, whether through illness, loss of job, loss of a loved one, stress, uncertainty, an adverse effect on lifestyle or social isolation.

We've written this book as a way to offer more tips and techniques into the ***how of happiness***, particularly using the benefits of recent research in our brain's amazing capacity to create patterns of thinking, feeling and behaving, often referred to as habits.

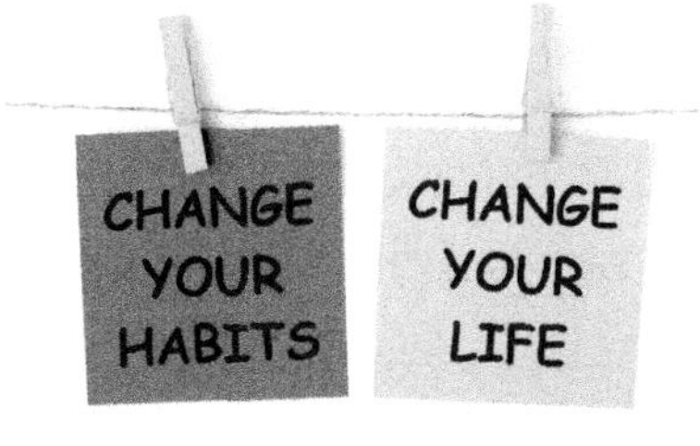

Because of our responses to Covid-19, our very clever brains have already begun to create new habits. For example, it's now acceptable and expected that we wear face masks in shops and do social distancing. Whenever we see a clip on TV, created before Covid-19, in which people are, for example, shaking hands or crowded together in a bar, it can strike us as strange and not normal at all. These observations led us to imagine how valuable it could be to understand and use the brain's amazing habit formation skills to create habits, built round the *science of happiness.*

Our brains very quickly and easily create new habits—for good or for bad. Repeat a behaviour a few times and it miraculously gets automated. For example, when we pick up a pen, we don't ever have to ask ourselves which hand to hold it in. We just do it automatically. At home recently, our dishwasher broke down; even though we knew it didn't work, we both often found ourselves putting dishes in it. Simply a matter of habit.

Habits are created by repeated tiny actions which may initially go unnoticed, but once they are embedded into our daily lives, they can have a big effect on shaping those lives. The good news is that we can use our brain's ability to do this and create positive habits which produce more happiness for ourselves, for others and for the world. That's why the subtitle of this book is *turning tiny steps into giant strides.*

"One tiny step at a time. . . .
Turning tiny steps into giant strides."

In the following chapters, we'll be exploring more of the most important components of happiness and how to build up positive habits in each of them. The components are:

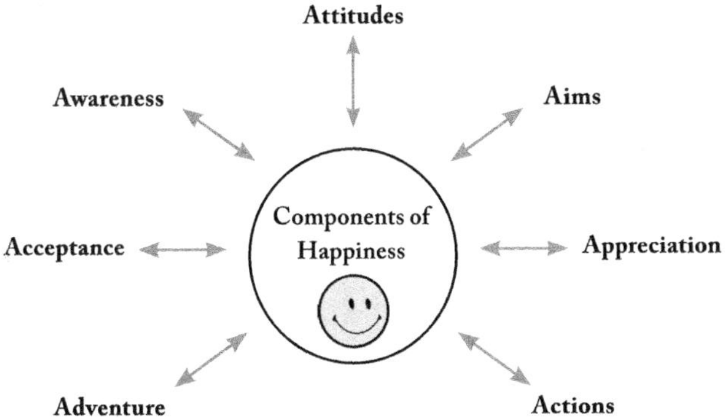

A good place to start is to find out more about the pioneering work of the *Action for Happiness* movement, which provides so many useful resources, information and tips about happiness. And that's where we're going next.

CHAPTER 1
THE ACTION FOR HAPPINESS MOVEMENT

In this chapter, we're going to explore the *Action for Happiness* movement which provides a number of useful resources, tools and networks promoting happiness. Their website is:

www.actionforhappiness.org

They promote *Ten Keys to Happier Living* which are based on the latest research in positive psychology, neuroscience, behavioural economics and biology. Their research evidence suggests these Ten Keys, once they are embedded into our lives, can have a significant and positive impact on our happiness and wellbeing. The Ten Keys are spelled out as *GREAT DREAM.* The first five keys (*GREAT*) are about our interaction with the outside world. The second five keys (*DREAM*) relate to our inner world and depend on our attitude to life.

Action For Happiness

Giving—Do things for others
Caring about others is fundamental to our happiness. Helping other people is not only good for them and a great thing to do, it also makes us happier and healthier too. Giving also creates stronger connections between people and helps to build a happier society for everyone. And it's not all about money—we can also give our time, ideas and energy. So, for example, we can give someone a smile as we pass them by on the street, or help an elderly person take out their rubbish bin.

Relating—Connect with people
Relationships are the most important overall contributor to happiness. People with strong and broad social relationships are happier, healthier and live longer. Close relationships with family and friends provide love, meaning, support and increase our feelings of self worth. Broader networks bring a sense of belonging. So, taking action to strengthen our relationships and create new connections is essential for happiness.

Exercising—Take care of our body
Our body and our mind are connected. Being active makes us happier as well as being good for our physical health.

It instantly improves our mood and can even lift us out of despondency. We don't all need to run marathons—there are simple things we can all do to be more active each day. We can also boost our wellbeing by unplugging from technology, getting outside and making sure we get enough sleep.

A 2018 study from the Karolinska Institutet in Stockholm, Sweden, suggests replacing time spent sitting with low intensity physical activity may benefit health more than previously thought. In the journal *Clinical Epidemiology*, the authors report how replacing half an hour of inactivity each day with housework, walking, standing, or similar low-intensity activity is linked to a 24% reduced risk of death from cardiovascular disease.

These findings might come as a pleasant surprise, especially to those who assume that only moderate or vigorous intensity physical activity can make a sizable difference.

AWARENESS—Live life mindfully

Mind Full, or Mindful?

Our minds are constantly *on the go*, often thinking about the past or the future. And this can be very tiring. But what about today? It can be easy to miss the joys and benefits of today. We need to stop and take notice; to be more mindful. Learning to be more mindful does wonders for our wellbeing in all areas of life. For example from simple things like a walk to the shops and the way we eat, or to more complex areas of life such as the quality of our relationships. It helps us get in tune with our feelings and stops us dwelling on the past or worrying about the future—so we get more out of the day-to-day.

Trying out—Keep learning new things

Learning affects our wellbeing in positive ways. It exposes us to new ideas and helps us stay curious and engaged. It also gives us a sense of accomplishment and helps boost our self-confidence and resilience. There are many ways to learn new things—not just through formal qualifications. We can share a skill with friends, join a club, learn something online, play a new sport, pick up a hobby we may have done in our younger years or branch out and do something completely new.

Recent Covid related lockdowns have provided opportunities for this. For example, research from global market research provider, Mintel, found that 55% of people cooked from scratch more since the pandemic, not least in making sour dough bread and banana cake.

Direction—Have goals to look forward to

Feeling good about the future is important for our happiness. We all need goals to motivate us and these need to be challenging enough to excite us, but also achievable. If we try to attempt the impossible this brings unnecessary stress. Choosing ambitious but realistic goals gives our lives direction and brings a sense of accomplishment and satisfaction when we achieve them.

Resilience—Find ways to bounce back

All of us have times of stress, loss, failure or trauma in our lives. How we respond to these has a big impact on our wellbeing. We often cannot choose what happens to us, but we can choose our own attitude to what happens. In practice it's not always easy, but one of the most exciting findings from recent research is that resilience, like many other life skills, can be learnt.

EMOTIONS—Focus on what's good

Positive emotions—joy, gratitude, contentment, inspiration and pride—are not just good at the time. Regularly experiencing them creates an upward spiral, helping to build our resources. So, although we need to be realistic about life's ups and downs, it helps to focus on the good aspects of any situation—the glass half full rather than the glass half empty.

ACCEPTANCE—Be comfortable with who we are

No-one's perfect. But so often we compare ourselves to other people. Dwelling on our flaws—what we're not, rather than what we've got—makes it much harder to be happy. Learning to accept ourselves, warts and all and being kinder to ourselves when things go wrong, increases our enjoyment of life, our resilience and our wellbeing. It also helps us accept others as they are.

MEANING—Be part of something bigger

People who have meaning and purpose in their lives are happier, feel more in control and get more out of what they do. They also experience less stress, anxiety and depression. Where do we find meaning and purpose? It might be our religious faith, being a parent or doing a job that makes a difference. The answers vary for each of us, but they all involve being connected to something bigger than ourselves.

The Action for Happiness movement operates local networks, each of which runs a range of courses and support to enable people to continue to learn and develop. We fully support everything Action for Happiness does and are involved with them locally.

In the last few years, as we've reflected on how people can achieve greater happiness in life, we've found ourselves focussing more and more on recent research about how the brain works and how we can use this research to help us to be happy in life. One area of research has focussed on how quickly and easily the brain creates habits (for good and for bad). In the next chapter, we'll explore how these insights can help us in our happiness quest.

CHAPTER 2
HOW OUR BRAINS WORK

The purpose of this chapter is to find out from neuroscience how our brains work to create habits. Once we're more aware of the lightning speed and efficiency with which our brains do this, we explore how we can make good use of this very special ability—leading to greater happiness in life.

First, we need to define what we mean by the word *habit*. The Cambridge English Dictionary defines it as:

> **"Something you do often and regularly, usually without knowing you are doing it."**

It's often said that we're all *creatures of habit* and in many ways, this can be a blessing. When we pick up a pen to write something, we don't first have to think about which hand to hold the pen. It just happens . . . as a matter of habit. Without habits, for example, a trip to the supermarket would take hours and be mentally exhausting. We would never remember where each item is kept and we would have to spend so much time hunting things out.

On the other hand, it's too easy to develop unhelpful or destructive habits, including procrastination, poor diet, poor sleep patterns, excessive over-spending and life threatening addictions. Our ability to create negative habits can often get in the way of our happiness as well as adversely affecting the happiness of others.

One of the best researchers on the way we humans create and live in accordance with our habits is James Clear, whose book *Atomic Habits* was published in 2018. He describes how in 2003, Dave Brailsford was hired as a coach by British Cycling. Within a few years, Brailsford had transformed the fortunes of elite British cycling, largely by encouraging the cyclists to make lots of tiny improvements in their riding and their training habits. The team were encouraged to make 1% improvements day by day. This resulted in Bradley Wiggins winning the Tour de France in 2008, followed by Chris Froome. The team then went on to win Olympic Gold medals in 2012.

In his book, James Clear attributes this dramatic success to Brailsford's understanding of the way continued tiny improvements in technique accumulate over time, resulting in a massive increase in performance.

If we pause and think about it, this is exactly how nature works, as one season gently morphs into the next one. And how does a tiny acorn grow into a mighty oak tree? An oak tree typically grows 0.3 metres each year until it's reached its full glorious height of approx 40 metres. It makes one small growth every day until it's realised its full potential.

Here's how the maths work. If you get 1% better each day for a whole year, you'll end up with performance which is 37 times better overall. Conversely, of course, if you get 1% worse each day for a whole year, you'll decline nearly down to zero.

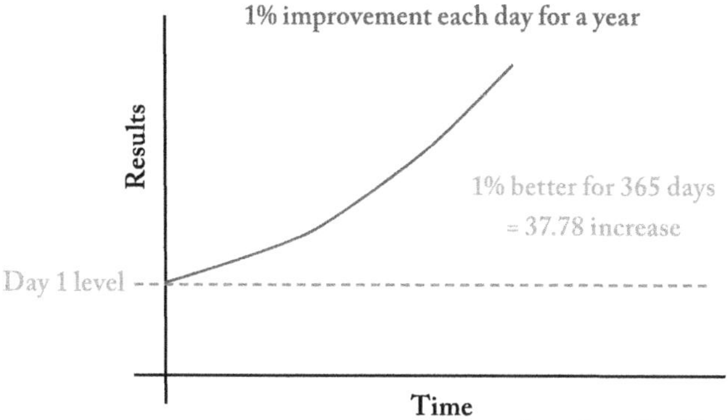

Source: James Clear "Atomic Habits"

As James Clear says:

> **"Habits are the compound interest of self improvement. The same way that money multiplies through compound interest, the effects of your habits multiply as you repeat them."**

These tiny changes seem at first to make little difference day by day, but over a period of a few months, add up to massive differences.

It's the same as saving a small amount of money each day, like many of us did as children with our piggy banks. Start small, saving £1 on a Monday, £2 on a Tuesday, £3 on a Wednesday and so on.

Sunday's saving is £7 and then you start again with another £1 on Monday.

If you'd started on January 1, you could have saved £1,456 by the end of the year.

This is sometimes called *the snowball effect*:

That's why the subtitle of this book is *Turning Tiny Steps into Giant Strides.*

However, in order to use the brain's ability to create habits so easily, it helps to understand more about how our brains work.

Our brains are the product of millions of years of evolution. From hundreds of million years ago, when the only life on the planet were reptiles, through to the times when the early mammals evolved, and up to the evolution of the human species.

As a consequence, our brains are made up of three interlinked and quite different segments:

- the lizard (or reptilian) brain
- the mammal (or limbic) brain
- the human brain.

The first brains appeared on the planet about 500 million years ago, when the only life on earth was reptiles. About 430 million years ago, the first mammals evolved and the reptilian brain slowly developed into the mammal brain. 70 million years ago, as the first early primates evolved, their brains began to develop higher level skills. At this point something happened which resulted in our brains doubling their mass and producing what we now recognize as the human brain. One of the consequences of this pattern of development has left our brains with some built in *design faults* where there are three distinct, but interconnected parts.

When we take account of the way our brains have evolved, starting with the lizard brain, we need to understand that the prime function of the strongest (and most ancient) parts of our brain is not to seek happiness, but rather to keep us safe from life threatening dangers such as wild animals, invasions from other tribes and starvation. Our brains are superb and operate with lightning speed at doing something most of us (gladly) no longer have to do, which is to be kept safe from being attacked, for example, by packs of hungry wolves.

THE LIZARD BRAIN

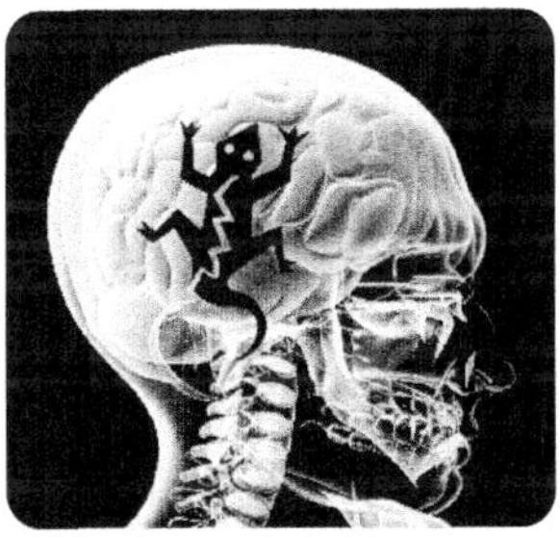

The lizard brain is located deep in our brain stem, is strongly linked to the spinal cord and is responsible for governing some of the most fundamental functions such as breathing, eating, sleeping, waking up, looking out for and responding to danger as well as basic survival.

The lizard brain doesn't learn well, preferring instead to operate *by instinct*, repeating the same basic survival responses over and over again.

Neuroscientists use the label *basal ganglia* to describe one of the most ancient parts of the lizard brain. In the 1990s, MIT researchers carried out a series of experiments on rats as they navigated their way out of a maze, to see to what extent the basal ganglia was the place in the brain which created and stored habits. The details of these experiments are described in Charles Duhigg's *The Power of Habit: Why We Do What We Do.* The evidence was overwhelming. These ancient parts of our brains are responsible for our fantastic skills in habit formation (regardless of whether the habits are good for us or not).

So, when you next do something on autopilot, such as writing a letter with your pen in one hand rather than the other, you'll now know this is a result of your most ancient part of your brain doing this automatically for you. And if you ever wonder how and why the brain can learn habits so quickly and so well, it's because it's had hundreds of millions to perfect the skill.

THE MAMMAL BRAIN
(SOMETIMES CALLED THE LIMBIC SYSTEM)

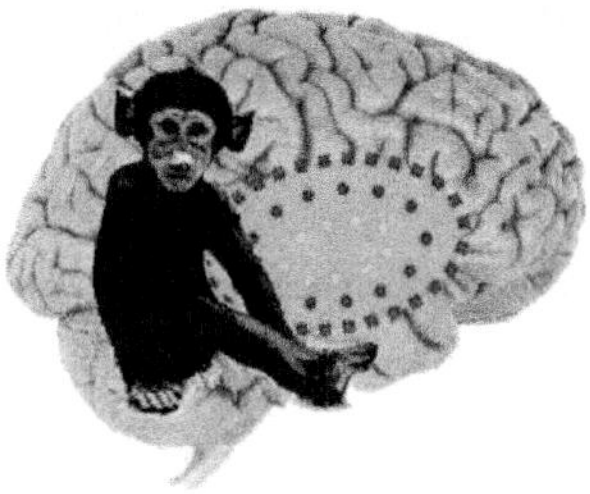

This part of the brain is unique to mammals. It's existed on the planet for approx 400 million years. According to Paul MacLean (1990), this part of the brain is the centre of emotion and learning. It developed very early in mammals to regulate the motivations and emotions that we now associate with feeding, reproduction and attachment behaviours. It's this part of the brain that governs our *fight or flight* behaviours. In MacLean's explanation, the limbic system evaluates everything as either agreeable (pleasure) or disagreeable (pain/distress). Survival is predicated on the avoidance of pain and the repetition of pleasure.

Dr Steve Peters is a consultant psychiatrist who specialised as an elite sports coach for many years, especially in his role as resident psychiatrist with the British Cycling Team from 2001. In his book *The Chimp Paradox,* written in 2011, he refers to the mammal brain as a *Chimp;* an emotional machine that resides in each of our heads, but one that tends to think independently from us. It constantly offers emotional thoughts and feelings that can be constructive or very destructive. It's not good or bad, it's just a Chimp. We're not responsible for the nature of the Chimp, but we are responsible for managing it.

For example, when something happens to us, such as when a family member drops some plates on the floor and they break into small pieces, we might find ourselves losing our temper.

But in the cold light of day, after we've resumed control of our inner Chimp's response, we may well realise that we may have over-reacted somewhat to a simple accident. The trouble is of course that we may in anger have said some things which leave a sour mark on family relationships for quite a while.

THE HUMAN BRAIN

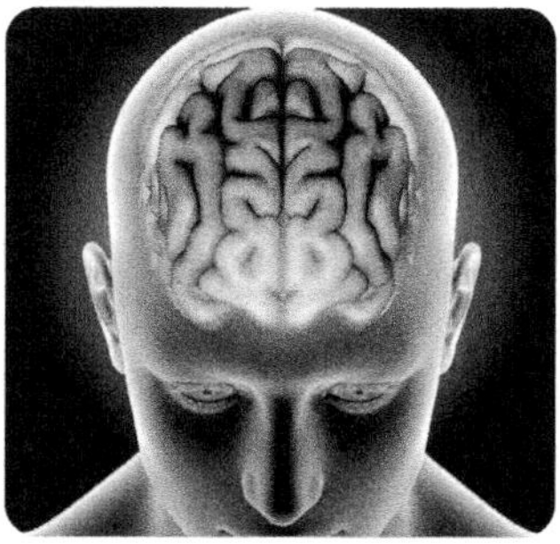

This is the youngest part of the brain (approx 70 million years old). It's also known as the neocortex and it's the part that differentiates us from other animals. It's in charge of planning, anticipating, perceiving time and context, making sense of emotions and giving us the ability to make conscious choices.

It would be good to think we always behave with the human brain firmly in charge, but sadly, this is not the case, especially when we've allowed the Chimp to take charge. For example, have you ever lost your temper and afterwards said something to yourself or to others like: *I completely lost it,* or *I don't know what came over me?* You're not alone. It's what we humans do and is part of our human experience. When the more ancient parts of the brain, i.e. the lizard or mammal brain take charge, our human brain can too often find itself sidelined, at least for a while, until the emotions generated by the mammal brain have subsided.

The extreme speed of flight or fight behaviours can save our lives if we find ourselves in a dangerous life or death situation, so thank goodness for them. However, as we all know, sometimes the most ancient parts of our brains respond in their automatic ways when they don't need to. For example, when we mislay our car keys and are in a hurry, we may wrongly accuse our partner or children of moving them from their normal place in the house. Or we see other people around us who lose it and it's tempting for our own brains to respond in kind, resulting in an argument with someone we love . . . but for no apparent, logical reason.

So, the key question is, how can we manage these 3 brains in our heads? First, it helps to understand in particular the following key aspect of our brain, i.e. when we learn, we change its structure.

Riding a bike seems impossible at first. But soon we master it. How? As we practice, our brain sends bike riding messages along certain pathways of neurons over and over again, forming new connections. In fact, the structure of our brain changes every time you learn, as well as whenever we have a new thought, our brains form new connections.

Try this:

1. Fold your arms. Which arm is on the top? Left or right arm?
2. Now repeat the exercise with the OPPOSITE arm on the top.

Does it feel strange? Of course. You're using a different set of skills. Repeat this unfamiliar way of folding your arms a dozen time. Does it feel any different? It may take you a few more repetitions but within a short space of time, this new way is as familiar as the old way. Your brain has learnt and in a very subtle and tiny way, has changed its internal structure. Below, are 2 further important insights from neuroscience about how the brain works.

EXERCISE HELPS MAKE US SMARTER

It's well known that any exercise that makes our heart beat faster, like running or playing basketball, is great for our body and can even help improve our mood. But scientists have recently learned that for a period of time after we've exercised, our body produces a chemical that makes our brain more receptive to learning. If we're stuck on a tricky problem, going out for a walk or just running upstairs before trying the problem again can lead to a solution.

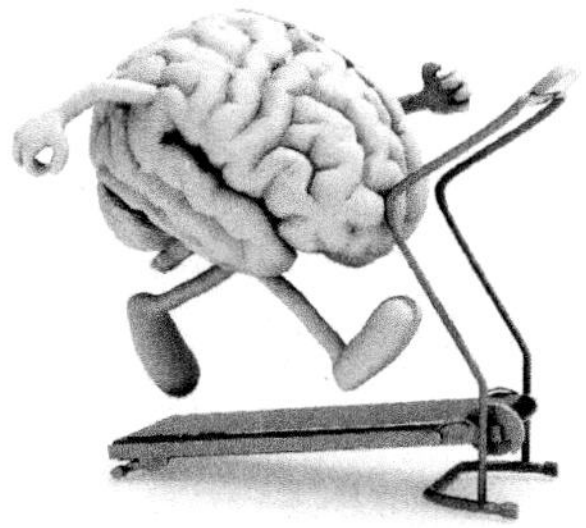

THE POWER OF THE UNCONSCIOUS MIND

Of all the activity that goes on in our brains, we're only conscious of about 10%. This is called the conscious mind. The other 90% of brain activity occurs below the surface of conscious awareness, in our unconscious mind. It's this part of the brain that drives our habits. For example, when we've sometimes driven to work, parked up and then paused to reflect on how we got there, it's our unconscious mind which has done it all for us through sheer force of habit. Imagine, for example, how difficult and time consuming it would be if every time we came across a door handle, we had to work out how to open it.

My Conscious and Unconscious Minds

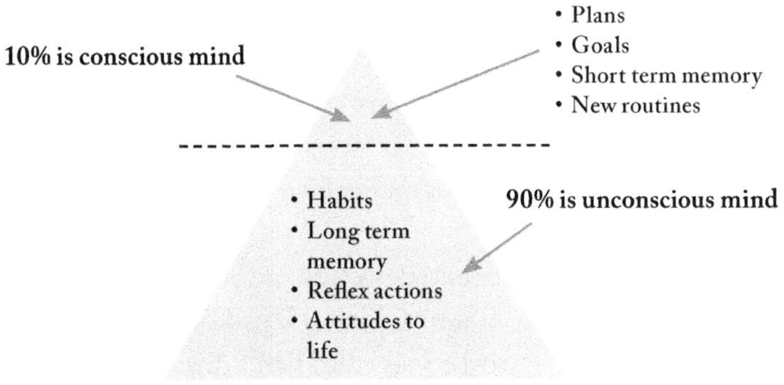

Much of what we do is driven not by conscious thought, but by *force of habit*, i.e. by unconscious thought. For example, when we stand up and walk, for most of us at least, we just do it without having to think. (Compare that with the image of a toddler who's walking for the first time). Of course, it's useful that our brains have the capacity to automate so much of what we do in life—thus freeing up our brain bandwidth for new ideas and behaviours.

It is however as easy to create unhelpful habits as it is to create helpful habits. In fact, given the welter of unending advertising that each person experiences each day and their focus on things that are often not good for our health and long-term wellbeing, it's probably easier for us to create more unhelpful habits than helpful habits.

A key aspect to being happy with good levels of health and wellbeing is to know how to harness the brain's ability to create habits that serve us well.

How do we do this? First, we need to create positive habits.

CREATING POSITIVE HABITS

We all know the power that habits can have in our lives and the lives of others. If we've ever commuted to work on the train, we may have spotted how so many of us tend to sit in the same compartment or how, given a choice of type of coffee drink, most of us automatically opt for the one we had last time.

One of the most influential doctors and writers on personal health is Dr Rangan Chatterji, who, in addition to being a practising GP, has worked as the BBC Breakfast health expert. In his book *Feel Better in 5: Your Daily Plan to Feel Great for Life,* Dr Chatterji refers to research that shows that at least 50% of all that we all do is driven by habits. As he says:

"We are our habits."

Another inspirational phrase he sometimes uses is:

"Your lifestyle can be your medicine."

He goes on to say that the key to health and wellbeing is to take tiny positive steps, each day. The ripple effect of these can help improve our general health and wellbeing. He suggests that we each take five minutes, three times a day, five days per week, to take small actions which are good for our mind, our body and our heart.

Dr Chatterji offers six top tips to help people to establish such new habits:

- start easy
- connect each health snack to an existing habit
- respect your own rhythm
- design your environment
- use positive self talk
- celebrate your success.

He suggests that we each take three (x five minutes) snacks a day:

- a mind health snack
- a body health snack
- a heart health snack.

Examples would be:

mind health snack	Reflecting on yesterday, what you achieved and what you learnt.
body health snack	Two sets of press ups or physical stretches.
heart health snack	Reflecting on your blessings and what you're grateful for.

Habits are driven from our unconscious minds and a key part of personal happiness is to harness this fantastic power. A good way to do is through making tiny but repeated positive habits in the way suggested by Dr Chatterji.

Another highly respected thinker on self development is Stephen Covey, who emphasises the role of using the positive power of good habits, in his bestselling book *The Seven Habits of Highly Effective People.* Covey's work focusses not on eliminating bad habits but on building up good ones. Changing our habits can change not only the way we see the world, but the way the world sees us. His work has lasted the test of time and has helped millions of people. His seven habits are:

1. Be proactive
2. Begin with the end in mind
3. Put first things first
4. Think win-win
5. Seek first to understand, then to be understood
6. Synergise
7. Sharpen the saw

Dr Covey has a useful website which contains lots of helpful tips at:

https://www.franklincovey.com

In conclusion, neuroscientists have shown that if we practice habits, the structure of our brain changes by growth in nerve cells and connections between them.

For example, imagine you have a well-established habit of going to the gym and staying there until your workout is complete. When you go the gym, the relevant brain cells recognise this is happening; and automatically communicate with the brain cells that know that you always stay until the workout is complete. The more you do this, the more these neurons connect with each other and the more they create a strong neural pathway between them. Hence the expression (Donald Hebb, 1949):

"Neurons that fire together, wire together."

It's like a river cutting through a valley; the longer it flows in the same path, the deeper and stronger that path becomes. That's how habits are made. All we have to do to create a new habit is to do something repeatedly.

Science now tells us that it takes the brain about three weeks to create strong new neural circuits, a new path for the river to take.

If you're interested to learn more about the neuroscience here, we include in the *References* a number of more detailed sources of information about how the brain does all this, so well and so very quickly.

In Summary

In this chapter, we've explored the brain's amazing skill and speed in creating habits, in the way we think, feel and behave—for good or ill. In particular, we've looked at:

- how the accumulation of tiny changes in how we think, feel and behave so easily and readily get stored and used at an unconscious level by our brains
- how the brain has evolved over millennia to do this exceptionally well
- how the brain's capacity to do all this can be used to create positive habits that bring us and others more happiness.

We hope this may have prompted some thoughts and questions in your mind and now would be a great time to pick up your pen, jot them down and capture them.

Neuroscience researcher, Dr Martin Lotze of the University of Greifswald in Germany, used fMRI scanners to explore which parts of the brain are used when we write down our thoughts on paper. The research shows that this habit can really help us create and develop new thinking. In other words, *thinking and inking.*

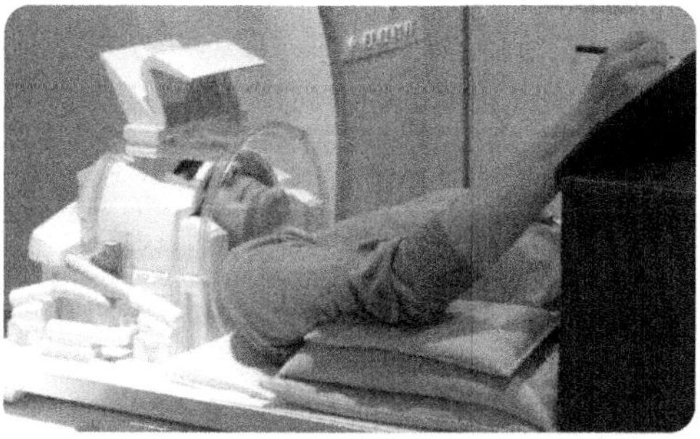

That's why many people are so committed to daily journaling, to help them reflect on their day or week and to help them plan their next day or week. In chapter 6, we talk about the proven benefits of writing a gratitude journal, as a way of helping them to appreciate the good things in life and take learnings from whatever happens to them in life.

Furthermore, writing notes adds a new perspective to things. Writing our thoughts down and sleeping on it allows us to see our original thoughts through new eyes, almost as if someone else had written them down.

The research showed that as people committed their thoughts in writing, some parts of the brain associated with vision became more active. In other words, when the research subjects were writing about their future aspirations, it's possible that they were in effect, seeing the scenes they were writing about, thus making it much more possible that the future aspirations would actually happen.

Also, a 2017 study in the journal *Frontiers in Psychology* found that brain regions associated with learning are more active when people completed a task by hand, as opposed to on a keyboard. The authors of that study say writing by hand may promote *deep encoding* of new information in ways that keyboard writing does not. Writing by hand may also improve a person's memory for new information.

And this is why, at the end of each main chapter, we invite readers to pause, reflect, pick up a pen and commit your thoughts to paper.

CHAPTER 3
ACCEPTANCE

In the last chapter, we reminded ourselves of how clever our brains are, in so many ways. They swiftly create habits, whether we like it or not. They also find an uncanny knack of focussing attention on either what happened yesterday, last week, last month or last year or what might possibly happen tomorrow, next week, next month or next year, rather than the now.

We also learnt in the last chapter how the human brain has evolved over thousands of years to keep us safe from danger. Part of the way it does this is by focussing our attention on possible threats and problems; all of which can lead us to ruminating and worrying. Furthermore, the reality of our daily lives often pulls us into the future, worrying about where we're going to find the money to pay the rent, how our children will do at school or whether our job will still be there in a few months' time.

Thinking about the future is an important part of happiness, but we need to do it in a helpful way, not in a way which causes anxiety and stress. Indeed, this tendency of our brains to ruminate and worry is probably one of the biggest contributors to our unhappiness.

In contrast, one of the most important habits of happiness is to be able to *accept* what is in our control; to *accept* what we cannot change and to *accept* (and appreciate) the realities of the present moment. There's so much wisdom in the following saying by the American thinker Reinhold Niebuhr:

> **"Grant me the serenity to accept the things I cannot change, the courage to change the things I can, and the wisdom to know the difference."**

Or as the Dalai Lama says:

> **"There are only two days in the year that nothing can be done. One is called Yesterday and the other is called Tomorrow. Today is the right day to Love, Believe, Do and mostly Live."**

The trick is to find a way of reflecting on the past and the future in a useful way while not missing out on the pleasures and happiness of the present moment. This is what many people would call *mindfulness.*

MINDFULNESS

One of the most prominent and recent pioneers in this field is Jon Kabat-Zinn, the American professor of medicine and the creator of the Center for Medicine and Mindfulness in Massachusetts, who defines mindfulness as:

> **"Mindfulness is awareness that arises through paying attention, on purpose, in the present moment, non-judgmentally."**

It's easy to stop noticing the world around us. It's also easy to lose touch with the way our bodies are feeling and to end up living in our heads, caught up in our thoughts without stopping to notice how those thoughts are driving our emotions and behaviour. An important part of mindfulness is reconnecting with our bodies and the sensations they experience. This means waking up to the sights, sounds, smells and tastes of the present moment. That might be something as simple as the feel of a banister as we walk upstairs or the rustle of the leaves in the autumn breeze. A second important part of mindfulness is an awareness of our thoughts and feelings as they happen moment to moment. It's about allowing ourselves to experience the present moment fully.

When we do that, it can positively change the way we see ourselves and our lives and enhance our wellbeing. Becoming more aware of the present moment can help us enjoy the world around us more and understand ourselves better. When we become more aware of the present moment, we begin to experience afresh things that we've maybe previously taken for granted. As Professor Williams, former director of the Oxford Mindfulness Centre writes:

> **"Mindfulness also allows us to become more aware of the stream of thoughts and feelings that we experience and to see how we can become entangled in that stream in ways that are not helpful."**

Gradually, we can train ourselves to notice when our thoughts are taking over and realise that thoughts are simply mental events that don't actually have to control us. Most of us have issues that we find hard to let go and mindfulness can help us deal with them more productively.

Here is some valuable and ancient wisdom on this theme:

> **"Do not be anxious about your life, what you will eat or drink, nor about your body. Look at the birds of the air, they neither sow nor reap. And which of you by being anxious can add a single hour to their life."**
>
> —www.bible.com

Mindfulness also helps us notice signs of stress or anxiety earlier and helps us deal with them better. It is recommended by the National Institute for Health and Care Excellence (NICE) to prevent depression in people who have had three or more bouts of depression in the past.

So how does anyone become more mindful?

There is advice from the NHS, blogs, courses to attend and YouTube clips but here, we've drawn up some simple steps to begin personal practice.

Notice what's going on inside	Reminding ourselves to take notice of thoughts, feelings, body sensations and the world around us. This is the first step to mindfulness. Even as we go about our daily lives, we can notice the sensations of things, the food we eat, the air moving past the body as we walk. All this may sound very small, but it has huge power to interrupt the *autopilot* mode we often engage day to day and to give us new perspectives on life.
Keep it regular	It can be helpful to pick a regular time—the morning journey to work or a walk at lunchtime—when we decide to be aware of the sensations created by the world around us.
Try something new	Trying new things, such as sitting in a different seat in meetings or going somewhere new for lunch, can also help us notice the world in a new way.
Free yourself from the past and future	Left to its own devices, the human brain tends to dwell on thoughts about the past, or to fixate on thoughts about the future. We need to notice such patterns in our own thinking and say something quietly about being more interested in the now rather than being trapped in the past, or pre-living the future.

Watch your thoughts	Many people find it difficult to practice mindfulness, largely because of the inevitable intrusion of lots of thoughts and worries that often come into our heads. Mindfulness isn't about stopping these thoughts, but rather as seeing them in a different way. For example, imagine standing at a bus station and seeing a stream of *thought buses* coming and going, without having to get on the buses and being taken away by them. Some people also find it easier to cope with an over busy mind if they do gentle yoga or walking.

Mindfulness meditation involves sitting silently and paying attention to thoughts, sounds, the sensations of breathing or parts of the body, bringing attention back whenever the mind starts to wander. Yoga and tai chi can also help with developing awareness of our thinking and breathing.

Further useful advice on mindfulness can be found on the internet, including the following NHS internet site:

www.nhs.uk/mental-health/self-help/
tips-and-support/mindfulness/

There's an abundance of ways to increase our mindfulness, but for many people, it can be a real challenge. There's no doubt that it's a habit and like so many techniques in this book, the key to successful habit creation is to start with small actions and do them repeatedly, slowly progressing and moving up the scale. Some people resist the idea of *meditation* (for a number of reasons), but the good news is that there are lots of other ways to achieve success here.

One of the most innovative and easy ways to increase our mindfulness is to use the superb quality of the camera on our mobile phones to notice, capture and share images of nature around us. Taking a photograph requires a certain amount of focused attention and appraisal of one's direct environment, which we might otherwise miss entirely. In Stroud, Gloucestershire, Ruth Davey runs a delightful organisation called *Look Again*:

www.look-again.org

Her company is now recognised by the NHS and many organisations in the field of arts, health, organisational and community development. Her work has also been evaluated by the University of Gloucestershire. Ruth says:

> **"Mindful photography is using our sight and the lens of a camera or smartphone as an anchor to help us become more consciously aware of the present moment. It is experiencing the process of creating photographs in a non-judgmental, compassionate way."**

The *Look Again* methodology uses a combination of the following:

- slowing down and having time for quiet and stillness
- connecting with nature
- using the Five Ways to Wellbeing: be active, connect, keep learning, give, take notice (developed by the New Economics Foundation, neweconomics.org)

- using secular mindfulness practices, focussing on the key attitudes of mindfulness: the beginner's mind, curiosity, gratitude, acceptance, patience, trust, non-judging, compassion, non striving, letting go
- applying the *Look Again* framework for using mindful photography to build resilience and revision the future using calm, curiosity, connection, creativity, celebration, courage, compassion
- applying the duty of care to ourselves, others and the planet
- practicing feedback, reflection and action.

If you're interested in learning more about the work of *Look Again*, we include in the References (under the names R Sumner, S Hughes and D Crone) the details of the University of Gloucestershire evaluation report.

And so, in fact, there are lots of ways to embed the habit of mindfulness and changing the focus of our attention. We conclude this chapter with another example.

In the village where we live, a small group of us take care in the spring, the summer and autumn to observe and make a note of the butterflies we each see in our gardens and in the local churchyard, which is maintained as a nature reserve. Each month, we share this data with each other and more widely in the village. We love doing it and it has now become a well engrained habit of watching out for not just butterflies, but all flying insects. A small and delicious hobby, which of course helps to raise awareness in the village of the critical role insects play in pollinating the plants around us. Here's an example of one of the butterflies we discovered last year in the meadows surrounding the village. It's called a *common blue*:

Until we started the butterfly watching, we had no idea that this little beauty existed here. Now, we now know it's very common and is found in a variety of habitats especially sunny sheltered spots. It likes to feed off clover plants in meadows. So, now when we're out walking in the summer, we look for it. More mindfulness can easily bring so much joy to us and the world, once we find a way of embedding it as a habit

CIRCLES OF CONTROL AND CONCERN

Much of mindfulness involves understanding what is and is not in our control. We conclude this chapter with some important insights from Stephen Covey who in his *Seven Habits of Highly Effective People*, reminds us of the importance, particularly when times get tough, of focussing on those things that are actually in our control and not worrying about things we cannot control. Stephen Covey has a useful model called *Circles of Concern* which contributes enormously to resilience and good quality thinking:

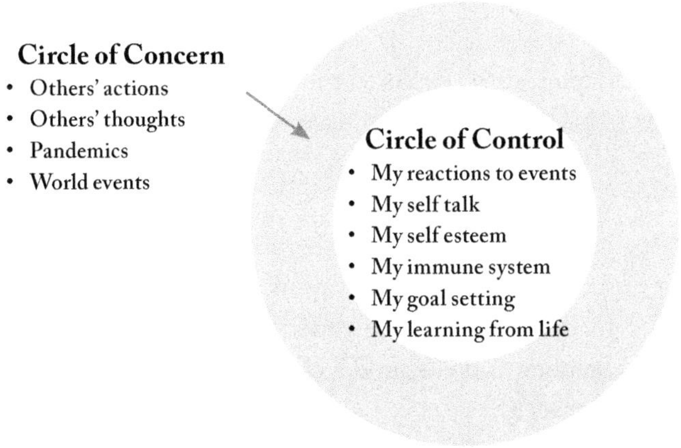

The key here is to focus our mind on the things that are in our own control (or influence) and not to waste energy, thoughts and precious time on things that are outside our circle of control.

In Summary

In this chapter, we've explored the theme of *acceptance* and the patterns that go with this. In particular, we've looked at:

- what mindfulness is
- its benefits
- some of the different ways it can be practised and made into a well embedded habit in our lives
- Stephen Covey's model of Circles of Control and Concern.

We hope this may have prompted some thoughts, questions or even some possible actions. Here's a quick nudge to pick up that pen or digital notepad, jot them down and capture them before we move onto the next chapter which is all about our habits around *Awareness.*

CHAPTER 4
AWARENESS

In this chapter, we explore some of the most critical aspects of happiness. Our awareness of:

- **what's going on inside ourselves**—our thoughts and our feelings and how we manage these
- **what's going on for other people**—their thoughts and feelings about things and how we can flex our own behaviours to strengthen our rapport with other people
- **the connections between our thoughts, our feelings and our actions**
- **our personalities**—how we prefer to think, feel and behave; and how we can, where appropriate, adapt our own behaviours to take account of others' personalities.

The more we're aware of these aspects of our lives and the better we manage them, the happier *we* will be and the happier *others* around us can be.

Have you ever noticed that some people are a joy to be with? Easy to get on with, comfortable in their own skin, good at managing their emotions, good at tuning into others and good at managing relationships? The best ones are also effective at putting their views across and can, in the right places, times and with the right people, be assertive and do what many of us find so challenging, which is to conduct difficult conversations well.

What marks them out from other people? The key word here is *awareness*. Awareness of:

- their own inner world
- their thoughts and emotions
- what's going on for others
- the relationships around them.

Some people call these skills a special kind of intelligence. There used to be a time when the word *intelligence* meant just one thing, which was how *clever* or *intellectual* a person is. Being intellectual can be helpful, especially if you're trying to solve a complex problem. But then Howard Gardner in his book *Frames of Mind*, published in 1983, suggested there's a range of different types of intelligences and that a person's talent can't be adequately represented by a single measurement, such as an IQ score.

EMOTIONAL INTELLIGENCE

In 1993, Peter Salovey and John Mayer, researchers at Yale University coined the term *emotional intelligence*. They described emotional intelligence as:

> **"The ability to monitor one's own and others' feelings and emotions, and to use this information to guide one's thinking and action."**

Since that time, the concept of emotional intelligence has been extensively researched and is a critical factor in our personal, family and work lives. Research by Maddocks and Hughes (2019) shows there are five key factors that contribute to emotional intelligence:

- paying attention to how others are feeling
- consulting and involving others where necessary
- investing time and energy in building relationships
- valuing individuals and respecting their views and opinions
- having faith in people whilst being realistic in expectations.

The following model of emotional intelligence is often used:

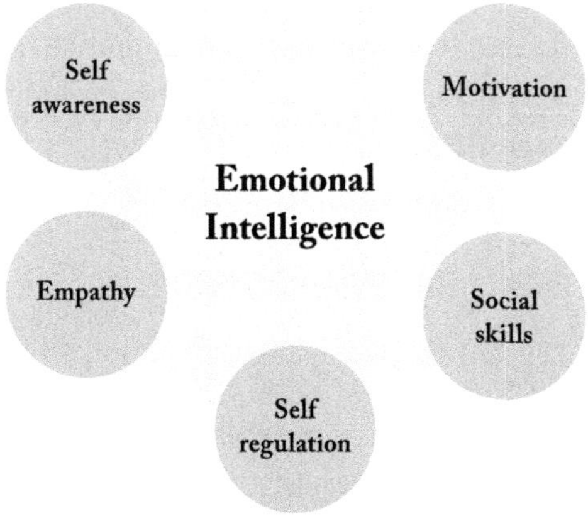

Self awareness	Self awareness is how conscious a person is of their own feelings and motives. Emotionally intelligent people often demonstrate a high level of self awareness. They know how their emotions affect themselves and others and they don't allow their emotions to control them.
Self regulation	People with the ability to self regulate don't make impulsive decisions. They pause and think about the consequences of an action before proceeding.
Empathy	Emotionally intelligent people are less likely to be self centred. Instead, they empathize with others and their situations. They tend to be a good listener, slow to judge and understanding of the needs and wants of others. For this reason, an emotionally intelligent person is often seen as a loyal, compassionate friend.

Social skills	It's easier for people with good social skills to collaborate and work in teams. They tend to be an excellent leader because of their strong communication skills and ability to manage relationships.
Motivation	People with emotional intelligence are productive and focus on the factors in their lives that they know are of most importance for them. They think about the big picture and assess how their actions will contribute to long-term success.

We suggest that these five factors are the essential ingredients for happiness whether at home, with family, with friends, in communities and organisations.

In chapter 2, we described how the ancient lizard brain is thousands of times faster and stronger than our human brain. Unless we're self aware and careful, we can find ourselves in situations where our reactions, driven by our ancient lizard brain, can completely take over and lead us to feel so angry and do stupid things which we later regret:

Emotional intelligence gives us the skills to deal better with such situations, so we manage our thinking and our emotions and thus take the right actions instead.

People with low levels of emotional intelligence may frequently experience some or all of the following situations:

- feel misunderstood
- get upset easily
- become overwhelmed by emotions
- have problems being assertive.

Whereas people with high levels of emotional intelligence often enjoy some of these situations:

- understanding the links between their emotions and how they behave
- remaining calm and composed in times of stress
- bouncing back well from adversity.

The good news is that our emotional intelligence skills aren't set down in stone when we're born. These skills are used and practised each moment in our lives, including when we're quietly sitting alone and thinking, as well as when we're interacting with others.

So, how do we go develop good habits of emotional intelligence? The first and probably the most important response here is to focus on our self awareness.

IMPROVING SELF AWARENESS

Self awareness is the ability to identify and understand our own emotions and the impact we have on others. It's the cornerstone of emotional intelligence and the other components of emotional intelligence depend on this self awareness. If we're aware of our own emotions and the behaviours they trigger, we can begin to manage these emotions and behaviours.

Emotions impact our mood, behaviours, performance and interactions with other people. We all experience different emotions all the time. The question is whether we're aware of these emotions and the impact they have on our behaviour and other people. People who are self aware tend to be more confident and more creative. They also make better decisions, build stronger relationships and communicate more effectively.

There are no *bad* emotions. All emotions can tell us something.

A trap people often fall into is thinking they *ought* to feel a certain way—that they are a *bad person* for feeling emotions they have been brought up to believe are wrong to express or even to have.

It's how we *respond* to those feelings that matters. Whatever emotion we're feeling, we still have a choice about how we act on it—and that's what counts.

Tips for increasing our self awareness

Tip 1

Whenever we feel an emotion we're not comfortable with, we can ask ourselves *what is this feeling trying to tell me?*

Tip 2

Take some time out to relax, being aware of your breathing as it flows in and out. Observe your thoughts and feelings as they come and go, without judging them. This will give you a degree of detachment, as you realise you're more than whatever thoughts and emotions you're experiencing at the time. You can see here the links with *mindfulness*, which we explored in the previous chapter.

IMPROVING SELF REGULATION SKILLS

Self awareness opens the door to self regulation, which is the ability to manage these emotions and behaviours. Once we're aware of our emotions, we can begin to manage them and keep the disruptive emotions and impulses under control.

People with strong self regulation can pause and take a deep breath in tense and stressful situations, which helps them remain calm and think before they speak or act.

These people tend toward a positive outlook and are adaptable to a variety of situations and circumstances. On the flip side, those that cannot contain their negative emotions and impulses often set off a chain reaction of negative emotions in others.

Tips for developing more self regulation

Tip 1

People can generally self regulate better if they pause and think objectively *in the cold light of day* about things before they take action. One of the best ways to do this is to sleep on things, knowing that the following day, we'll generally have a more objective perspective about things.

Tip 2

Another good way to become better at self regulation is to keep a daily journal. Just take five minutes each morning to write down how you're feeling. Writing things down in this way gives you a degree of detachment and allows you to express your feelings in a way which is safe. It also allows you to recognise recurring patterns in your emotional responses and gives you a record of how far you have come as you develop your emotional intelligence.

IMPROVING EMPATHY SKILLS

Empathy is our ability to understand the emotions of others—identifying what others feel, being sympathetic to this emotion and wishing to help and support other people in what they're experiencing. It's not about how we would feel in their situation, but rather, how others actually feel.

It's sometimes said that we should treat others as we would wish to be treated and there's some value in this. But there's certainly even more value in treating others *as they would wish to be treated.*

Any time we're dealing with another person—on a date, in a job interview, in a dispute, selling to them, or working with them, things will go more smoothly if from time to time we put ourselves in their shoes and ask ourselves, questions such as: *What's going on for this person right now? What's important to them? What do they want from this interchange? What might they be thinking and feeling?*

Everyone experiences the world in different ways and everything that a person does and says makes sense from their viewpoint, even if it makes no sense to us. People make the best choices they can, given how they see the world. If we assume others experience life as *we* experience it, then some of the actions they take might even seem, from our point of view, stupid or malicious. But if we can get a sense of what's going on for them, we'll find them much easier to understand and communicate with them.

People with strong social awareness tend toward kindness as well as being tough and fair. They often have the gift of being able to give others difficult feedback—in fact, they may be better at delivering this *tough love* because they understand the other person and want to help them improve.

Tips for developing empathy skills

Tip 1

Stepping into the shoes of other people and attempting to see things as they see things is one of the best ways to develop empathy skills.

Tip 2

Stephen Covey in his *7 Habits of Highly Effective People* includes as one of his 7 habits to *Seek First to Understand Before Being Understood.* This simple but powerful thought, once put into practice, goes a long way to develop the skills of empathy.

IMPROVING SOCIAL SKILLS

Finally, the development of more emotional intelligence also depends on our social skills.

The term *social skills* refers to a broad range of behaviours that, when in place and applied well, allow good quality interaction and communication between people. They include:

- influencing others
- listening to others
- stepping into others' shoes
- team working
- managing conflict
- motivating and inspiring others
- flexing our own behaviours to help others.

People with such skills can make an enormous difference in a team and in organizations because they understand others and act on this knowledge to move people toward a common goal.

Someone once said these wise words:

"Look after relationships and tasks generally look after themselves."

And of course, in relationships, it's often the tiny things that matter most. These habitual, tiny things in our lives show in a real and practical way how much we value our relationships with others.

Tips for developing more social skills

Tip 1

Ask yourself what your most important relationships are in life and then make a point of doing something, possibly a small action, which shows that you value that relationship.

Tip 2

Take action on any of the above other aspects of emotional intelligence and you will find there will be an automatic increase in the quality of the relationships around you.

Tip 3

Later on in this book, (in chapter 9), we talk about the wonderful value of taking a *Random Act of Kindness* each day. It's worth a try and a lovely habit to nurture.

IMPROVING MOTIVATION SKILLS

We can so easily lose sight of what's most important in life. Indeed, even in the good times, many of us may not realise what's most important to us and others; what most motivates us and them. It's as if we need an inner compass to remind us of what's most important. When we know what's most important about our lives and remind ourselves of this from time to time, it helps us to see things in the right perspective.

Tips for developing more motivation skills

Tip 1

In chapter 7, (on *Aims*), we include an exercise which helps people to surface the factors that are most important to them; the equivalent of their internal compass. Some people are fortunate to know instinctively what's most important to them. For many others, doing a short and simple exercise like this can help us enormously to clarify what most motivates us.

Tip 2

Another important way we can understand better what motivates us (and others) is to gain more insight into our personalities. There are several different well researched and valid models of personality that you can explore on the internet or in books. In the final part of this chapter, we include an overview of one such model *Insights Discovery* and we recommend this as a really useful starting point to help us understand ourselves and others even better.

Emotional intelligence questionnaire

If you'd like more information and might even like to take an online assessment of your current emotional intelligence strengths and possible areas of development, here's a link to an excellent source of such information:

www.psionline.com/en-gb/emotional-intelligence

Another way of looking at emotional intelligence is to see the interconnections between these three factors:

- what we think
- how we feel
- how we act.

THE MIND BODY CONNECTION

If we think of sucking a lemon, we may feel our mouths becoming uncomfortable. On the other hand, if we start thinking about our favourite food, we can find our mouths salivating. If we stand tall, inhale deeply and stretch our arms up towards the sky, we can feel more energised, whereas, if we walk along the road slouching, we can feel our internal mood declining. At the heart of all these interconnections is of course our amazing brain. Each of these factors affects the others, as illustrated in this diagram:

Mind and Body Connection

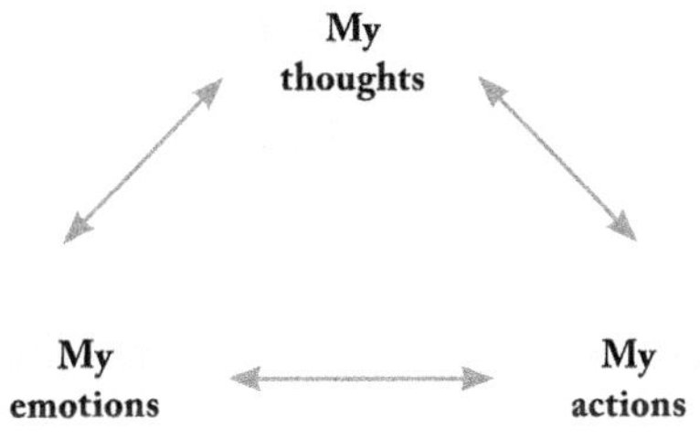

Even something as simple as how we breathe can impact on our wellbeing. This explains the growing impact of practices such as yoga on people's health and happiness. Equally, what we think in our heads impacts on the body. For example, when we imagine a situation, the brain reacts as if the thing we're imagining is really happening. And so, the thoughts we allow to pass through our brains can have a significant impact on the entire nervous system. If we think positive thoughts, their effect can be to relax automatically all of the body's systems. Equally, if we think negative thoughts, the opposite is true and we can create stress in our bodies.

There is so much neuroscience research now (for example by Lisa Feldman Barrett, University Professor at Northeastern University, America) which shows that in every moment of our life, our brains regulate the insides of our body, including our organs, hormones and immune system, to keep us alive. The process is like running a household budget, but instead of money, our brain budgets water, salt, hormones, glucose and other bodily resources as we gain and lose them. Actions that spend resources, such as exercise or stressful conversations, are like withdrawals from our account. Actions that replenish resources, such as eating, sleeping and cuddling a beloved pet are like deposits.

Finally, as we've said earlier in this chapter, another valuable way to increase our emotional intelligence is by understanding our own and others' personality better.

UNDERSTANDING PERSONALITY

Today, we often try to describe and assess the personalities of the people around us. *She has such a great personality,* you might say about a friend. *He gets his personality from his dad* you might say about your son. We spend a lot of time talking or thinking about personality, but what exactly is it?

There are a number of well researched models of personality—all of which add something to help us understand one of the most intriguing of issues, which is how human being think, behave and interact with each other and the planet.

Here, we'd like to focus on just one of these models, which is called *Insights Discovery*. This model is based on the work of one of the most influential people to shed light on the mysteries of our personalities, the Swiss psychologist Carl Jung (1875–1961).

Carl Jung suggested that our personalities are based on the interaction between a number of factors, including:

FACTOR	**DESCRIPTION**
Introversion	People with a preference for *Introversion* like to work alone or in small groups, using a more deliberate pace, focussing most on a few tasks at a time.
Extroversion	People with a preference for *Extroversion* are energised by people, enjoy a variety of tasks, a quick pace and are usually good at multi-tasking.
Thinking	People with a preference for *Thinking* usually base their views on logic and the data in front of them. They weigh up the pros and cons of situation using the facts and the logic. They most value honesty, fairness and consistency.
Feeling	People with a preference for *Feeling* have a thinking style which readily takes account of their own and others' values; and takes account of how people feel about something. Their views about situations often take account of how others may react to and feel about them.

In the early 1990s, a psychologist called Andi Lothian developed a powerful model of personality based around Jung's factors. He carried out extensive research to develop his model and without doubt, it provides useful insights into personality.

In doing all this, he had 3 ambitions which were to:

- increase people's understandings of themselves and others
- help people connect more strongly with each other
- provide a common language for people to communicate and relate to each other.

He called this the *Insights Discovery* model. Full details of it can be found at:

www.insights.com

The research showed that Jung's factors often combine into 4 major patterns, as illustrated below:

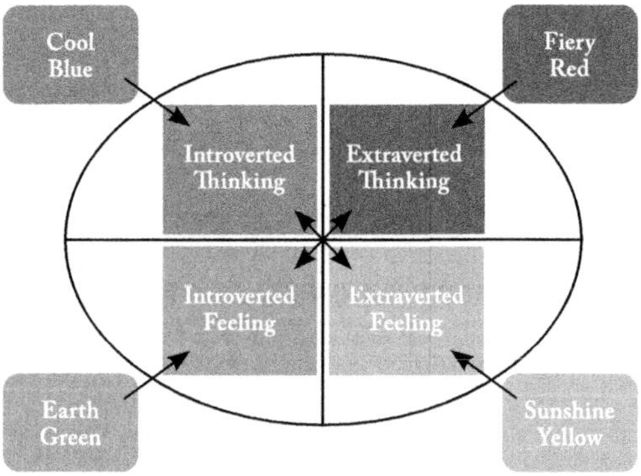

We each have all four patterns within us. It's the combination that creates the unique individual.

The research shows that we each have a preference for one or more of these combinations in how we respond to the world.

Here are some more details of the typical behaviours of each pattern:

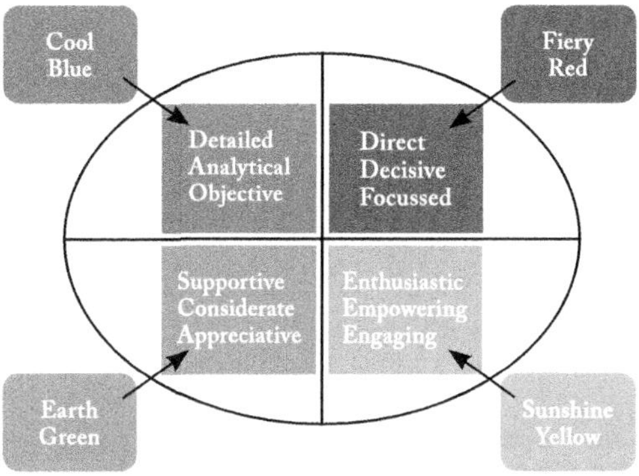

So, on a good day, a person with a dominant *Cool Blue* preference (an introverted and logical way of living) will tend to:

- pay attention to detail
- be objective and logical.

A person with a dominant *Fiery Red* preference (an extraverted and logical way of living) will tend to:

- be action orientated
- be direct and determined to make things happen.

A person with a dominant *Sunshine Yellow* preference (an extraverted way of living, led more from the heart) will tend to:

- be enthusiastic and dynamic
- be naturally empowering of others.

A person with a dominant *Earth Green* preference (an introverted way of living, led more from the heart) will tend to:

- be naturally considerate
- be sensitive to others' feelings and views about things.

It's often said though, that an overdone strength can be a big weakness and we all sometimes have a *bad day*, when there is too much to do and too much stress around. The *Insights* model tells us that on a *bad day*, our natural preferences can result in something more like this:

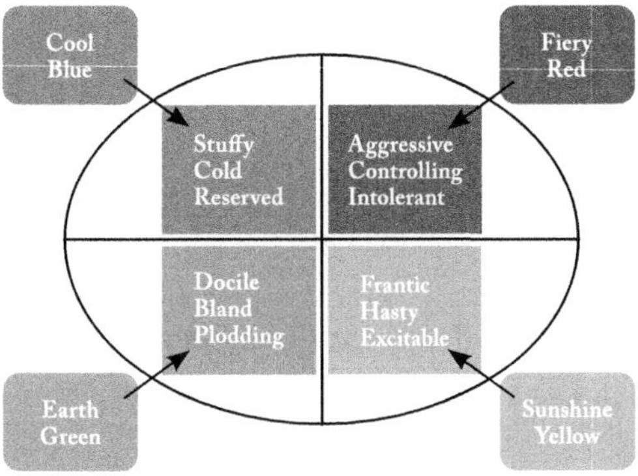

So, how do you stack up against this model? If you wish, you can complete the full questionnaire and get a full report, together with full feedback from a qualified practitioner in the Insights model, via www.insights.com.

Alternatively, there are a number of shortened and free questionnaires which give you a glimpse of how you map onto the *Insights* model. One of the sources is a Dutch company called *Bemotion*:

www.bemotion.nl/insights-kleurentest/
free-personality-color-test

When we have more awareness of what makes us and others tick, the world becomes a much better, happier place. Or to put it another way, as Carl Jung himself once said:

> **"Everything that irritates us about others can lead to an understanding of ourselves."**

In Summary

In this chapter, we've explored issues around our habitual patterns of *awareness*, in particular:

- the key importance of emotional intelligence for our happiness
- the 5 core aspects of emotional intelligence which are self awareness, self regulation, empathy, social skills and motivation
- the mind—body connection, i.e. the links between how we think, how we feel and how we act
- the value of gaining insights into our own personality and seeking to understand how other people may be similar to or different from you.

We hope all this has prompted some thoughts, questions and even possible actions. Now would be a great time to treat yourself to a nice coffee/tea break, pick up a pen, jot down and capture your thoughts/questions/actions, before we move onto the next theme which is the attitudes and beliefs we carry around and so often shape our lives.

CHAPTER 5

ATTITUDES AND BELIEFS

> **"We must look at the lens through which we see the world, as well as the world we see. And the lens itself shapes how we interpret the world."**
>
> —Stephen Covey

We instinctively know that different people often see things differently.

How we perceive the world and our place in it is partly chosen for us by our parents, our family, the media, our teachers and friends. The lens we use to see the world fundamentally shapes our attitudes and beliefs about the world, ourselves and others. For most of us, all this becomes a deeply embedded habit. If we're fortunate, the lens other people provide for us is a helpful one. Sadly, this is not always the case.

Many of our beliefs and attitudes to our lives have been inherited over hundreds of years. For example during the Middle Ages, many people thought the earth was flat until Magellan successfully circumnavigated the planet. Other beliefs that we commonly share are much more recent. For example, that one can't survive without wifi . . .

But as all photographers know: *change the lens and you change the thing you see.*

Another way of saying this is to quote Alfred Korzybski: *The map is not the territory.*

Here's an example of what he meant.

We're all familiar with the map of the London Underground:

Of course, the map bears no resemblance at all to what it's like on a London Tube train. When we think of something, we're making a representation of it in our heads and this representation may or may not be a 100% accurate description of the thing we're thinking about.

Why does all this matter?

Most of our core beliefs and attitudes operate at an unconscious level. Sometimes, it can serve our happiness if we surface them, review and change them to something more useful to us, others and the world.

Martin Seligman, one of the world's leading neuroscientists, has written extensively on this topic. In *Learned Optimism*, he reminds us that in much of the so-called developed world, there's an unprecedented epidemic of depression, particularly among young people, which our recent experience with Covid-19 has exacerbated.

A recent report by the Mental Health Foundation in the UK shows that:

- every week, 1 in 6 adults experiences symptoms of a common mental health problem, such as anxiety or depression
- 1 in 5 adults has considered taking their own life at some point
- nearly 50% of adults believe that, in their lifetime, they have had a diagnosable mental health problem, yet only 33% have received a diagnosis
- women between the ages of 16 and 24 are almost 3 times as likely (at 26%) to experience a common mental health problem as their male contemporaries (9%) and have higher rates of self-harm, bipolar disorder and post traumatic stress disorder
- another group at particular risk includes people in mid-life, with a noticeable increase in the prevalence of common mental health problems for both men and women between the ages of 55 and 64.

In America, a report written in 2020 from Blue Cross Shields (which looked at medical health insurance claims from 41 million insurance holders) found that major depression is on the rise among Americans from all age groups, but is rising fastest among teens and young adults.

What's behind the increase?

In the Blue Cross Shields report, Dr. Laurel Williams, chief of psychiatry at Texas Children's Hospital says: *Many people are worried about how busy they are. There's a lack of community. There's the amount of time that we spend in front of screens and not in front of other people. If you don't have a community to reach out to, then your hopelessness doesn't have any place to go.*

The report concludes by saying that diagnoses of major depression have risen dramatically by 33% since 2013.

The issues which cause these outcomes are complex, involving a mixture of factors such as genetics, medical conditions as well as the deep seated attitudes and beliefs we hold about the world.

Much of the power of Martin Seligman's research arises from his focus on the fundamental beliefs and attitudes we hold to be true about our lives and the world. He draws the distinction between *learned helplessness* and *learned optimism.* In other words, whether our basic attitude to life is that we:

- do (or don't) have choices in the way we lead our lives
- can (or can't) be pro-active and take control of key aspect of our lives
- can (or can't) learn to bounce back from adversity.

For example, Seligman's research shows that the way we think, especially about our health, actually changes our health. Optimists catch fewer infectious diseases than pessimists. Our immune system may work better when we're optimistic and optimists live longer than pessimists.

In other words, our attitudes and beliefs can often become self-fulfilling prophecies. An example of the self-fulfilling prophecy is known as the *placebo effect.* The placebo effect has been recognised in the medical world since at least 1799, when it was used by the English physician John Haygarth to secure improvements in patients' health.

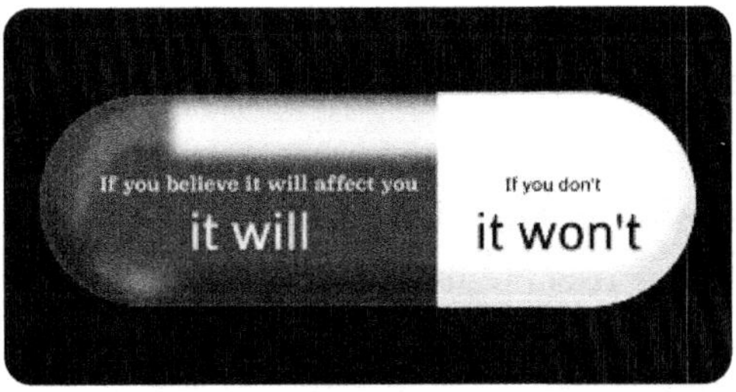

There are now many well researched cases of the self-fulfilling nature of the placebo effect in some patients. For example, the *JAMA Psychiatry Journal 2015* reports on one experiment when patients in a health care setting were randomly split into two groups, one receiving a new treatment and the other receiving a placebo treatment or *fake treatment*. In scientifically based trials, those people who are given the placebo drug often display improvements in the health issue, despite there being no active agent causing the recovery. Rather, it's *their beliefs* that lead to the prophecy being fulfilled.

Anther powerful example of the power of our beliefs and attitudes in significantly changing outcomes in life is the so-called *Pygmalion effect*.

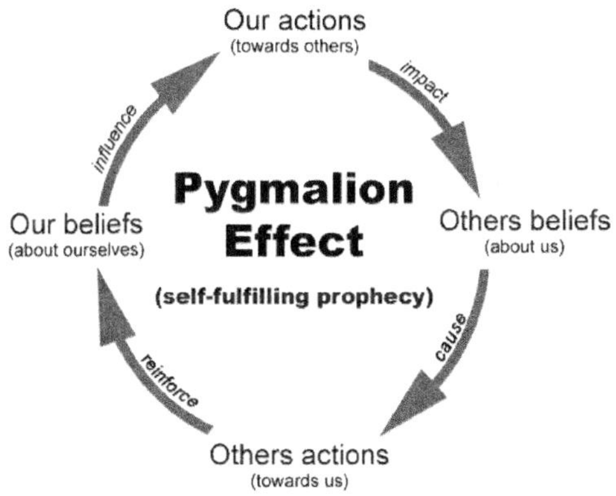

In 1968, researchers Rosenthal and Jacobsen conducted an experiment to see whether student achievement could be self-fulfilling, based on the expectations of their teachers.

Rosenthal and Jacobsen gave primary school children an IQ test and then informed their teachers which children were going to be average and which children were going to be high achievers. They gave the name *Bloomers* to the high achieving group.

They found that the teachers did not expect as much from the average children and gave all the attention to the *Bloomers*. The teachers created a more pleasant environment for the *Bloomers*, gave them more time and attention, called on them for answers more often and provided them with more detailed feedback when they got something wrong.

However, unknown to the teachers, these students were selected randomly and may or may not have fulfilled the IQ criteria. After eight months, they came back and retested the children's intelligence.

The results showed that the *Bloomers*', (the experimental group), IQ scores had risen significantly higher than the average students (control group), even though these academic *Bloomers* were chosen at random. The *Bloomers* gained an average of two IQ points in verbal ability, seven points in reasoning and four points in overall IQ.

The experiment showed that teacher expectations worked as a self-fulfilling prophecy. The teachers' expectations had altered the way the children were treated and this had affected their performance.

Over 30 years ago, Dr Carol Dweck (from Stanford University, USA) and her colleagues became interested in students' attitudes about failure. They noticed that some students rebounded while other students seemed devastated by even the smallest setbacks. After studying the behaviour of thousands of children, Dr. Dweck coined the terms *fixed mindset* and *growth mindset* to describe the underlying beliefs people have about learning and intelligence. When students believe they can improve, they understand that effort makes them stronger, they put in extra time and effort and that leads to higher achievement. The following diagram illustrates the main features of each mindset:

What Kind of Mindset Do You Have?

- I can learn anything I want to.
- When I'm frustrated, I persevere.
- When I fail, I learn.
- I want to challenge myself.

- I'm either good at it or I'm not.
- When I'm frustrated, I give up.
- When I fail, I'm no good.
- I don't like challenge.

Recent advances in neuroscience have shown us that the brain is far more malleable than we ever knew. Research on brain plasticity has shown how connectivity between neurons can change with experience. With practice, neural networks grow new connections, strengthen existing ones and build insulation that speeds transmission of impulses. These neuroscientific discoveries have shown us that we can increase our neural growth by the actions we take, such as developing positive habits, asking questions, practicing and following good nutrition and sleep habits.

At the time these neuroscientific discoveries were gaining traction, the same researchers began to understand the link between mindsets and achievement. It turns out, if you believe your brain can grow, you behave differently. So, the researchers asked, *Can we change mindsets? And if so, how?*

This began a series of interventions and studies that *prove we can indeed change a person's mindset from fixed to growth* and when we do, it leads to increased motivation and achievement. For example, teenagers who were taught that intelligence is malleable showed a clear increase in maths grades.

In addition to teaching young people about malleable intelligence, researchers started noticing that teacher behaviour has a big impact on student mindset and the feedback that teachers give their students can either encourage a child to choose a challenge and increase achievement or look for an easy way out. For example, studies on different kinds of praise have shown that praising hard work and effort cultivates a growth mindset. When students have a growth mindset, they take on challenges and learn from them, therefore increasing their abilities and achievement.

And of course, if children can change their mindsets, so too can adults. But how, specifically?

There are several ways we can each do this, if we choose. Here are 5 tips to consider, all on the creation of new habits in how we think:

Tip 1 for changing mindsets: questions we routinely ask ourselves

Possibly one of the best ways to do this is to create a habit, whereby we routinely ask ourselves questions such as:

1	What was my biggest challenge today? How did I do? How could I have done better?
2	What did I achieve today? If I could have the day again, how could I have done even better?
3	What did I learn from today? What mistakes did I make today and what do I learn from them?
4	How can I use today's learnings in the future?
5	What do I intend to achieve in the next week or day?
6	What feedback did I get today about how I did? How will I respond to this feedback?

Some people find it easier to track such changes and questions in a daily journal and there's great merit in doing this.

One of the themes of this book is to start small and create positive habits from small, repeated actions. In this spirit, if the least that we do, as we lie awake in bed at night is to ask ourselves just one or two of such questions, we can be surprised to discover after only a week or so, that our mindset has shifted in the right direction.

Another of the benefits of habitually asking ourselves questions of this sort is an improvement in the quality of our self talk.

Tip 2 for changing mindsets: changing our self talk

Most of us are in constant mental chatter, although much of it is not in our conscious awareness. It might, though, suddenly pop out of our mouths and become conscious when we do something like dropping a plate on the floor and we find ourselves using an expletive! Or it might be something of the kind illustrated below:

We talk to ourselves all day long and, unfortunately, such self talk can be negative. Often, it can be tainted with guilt about our past or anxiety about our future. This negativity can destroy any seed of hope that we may otherwise have in striving for our dreams. Our actions are inspired by our thoughts. If we can change the way we think, we can begin to change the actions we take. Practicing positive self talk can help us set in motion actions that will bring us greater rewards.

The following are three steps to positive self talk. By following these steps you'll begin to rid your inner conversations of negativity and instead have empowering thoughts. This should make it easier for you to achieve your goals. After all, no one wants to set out on changes and be bombarded with thoughts such as *I'll fail. I'll never do this. It's too hard.* We're sure you can insert many more from your own experience. The first step in dealing with this negative self talk is to become aware of it. Once we're more aware of it and if we notice any internal negative chatter, we can change it to something more useful.

A common negative talk involves saying *I can't.* When we say this or *it's too difficult*, we're creating a resistance. Having such a mental block will prevent us from completing a task we could otherwise achieve. Anytime we catch ourselves saying *I can't . . .* we need to turn around and challenge this claim with, *Why can't I?*

It may though not be easy to make a switch if we have a long history of negative self talk, i.e. it's become a habit. Our self talk has probably become negative over the years due to various factors. For instance, if our first teachers repeatedly told us we were stupid, it'll be hard not to believe them. Our inner chatter will be filled with talk of *I'm so slow* and *It's so hard to learn.* If we voice such negative stories, our actions are going to result in low self esteem. If we notice anything in our self talk which puts ourselves down, such as, *Typical of me* or *Why am I so stupid?* one option is to use the power of affirmations.

Affirmations are positive statements of a desired outcome or goal. They are usually short, believable and focussed. By repeating them over and over again, we build inroads into our unconscious mind, opening up the possibility of a new state of thoughts. An important step when repeating affirmations is to read the affirmations aloud with feeling. The mere reading of the words bears no consequence unless we put some emotions behind them. Why? Our unconscious mind takes any orders given in complete faith. So, the daily practice of repeating affirmations is important. Initially we may be sceptical toward the statement of the positive affirmation. However, if we follow this simple set of instructions, scepticism will soon give way to a new set of beliefs and then become crystallized into absolute faith.

Tip 3 for changing mindsets: creating a positive script for ourselves

And here's another thing about negative self talk. It can, over time, spin a drama that traps and limits us in life. Here's an alternative. Create an uplifting story that runs like a movie script. Some visualization will help here, (by which we mean to create a picture in our head of what we want our life to be like and imagine in our mind's eye that it's really happening).

Build on a story with a positive outline. The longer we can tell this story to ourselves, the better. It's also best if we can make this story about having our goals achieved. When we do this, we start to internalize our goals and dreams, as if they are something already achieved.

Not only will using positive self talk help us to achieve our goals and more happiness, it will also help us to bounce back when things go wrong, to be resilient, if you like.

Tip 4 for changing mindsets: creating a resilient mindset

Resilience is a quality we all need in life. It's the ability to bounce back from adversity, ideally learn from the bad times and do better next time. Our mindset and attitudes to life can though too often be non resilient.

A non resilient mindset may contain some or all of the following elements:

Non Resilient Mindset

"Oh no, I've made another mistake . . ."

This ruins everything.	**PERVASIVE**
I'll never get anywhere now.	**PERMANENT**
Just shows how useless I am.	**PERSONAL**

On the other hand, the kinds of things a resilient person will say to themselves are:

Resilient Mindset

"Oh no, I've made another mistake . . ."

What must I do differently?	LEARNING
I need to get more feedback.	ACTION
It's down to me to do better.	ACCOUNTABLE

In other words, a resilient person will have a different internal mental landscape, based on learning, action and personal accountability. There's a link here with emotional intelligence which we covered in chapter 4. One of the most effective ways to shift towards a more resilient mindset is to keep a daily journal and make a note of issues such as:

- what we need to do better next time
- what we learnt from the previous day or week
- the tiny things to do more of next time, until they become habits in the way we think and in our mindset.

We conclude this chapter with another really simple and powerful technique to help us to see things differently and to change our attitudes and beliefs where it is useful to do so. This is the technique known as *reframing*.

Tip 5 for changing mindsets: reframing

Reframing is another way to increase the perspectives we use to see the world. It's an invaluable technique of being able to change the frame we put round things and the exact frame we use can have a dramatic difference to how we think about the issue. The classic reframe that we all know is when we see a partly consumed beer glass; is it half full or half empty? There's probably a well rooted belief in our culture that our thoughts can't, don't or won't change. Have you ever heard someone say things like, *That's me. It's just the way I am.* They are mistaken. The more self aware we are, the more we know that we can, to an extent, choose or modify how we think about things, especially using this technique of changing the frame we use around our thoughts, i.e. reframing.

Frames are a major part of the system of filters through which we represent things internally. They act as mental templates or patterns, through which we experience the world. The frame we set, consciously or unconsciously, reflects the way we perceive things. *Reframing* means changing the frame of reference around a behaviour, statement or event, finding another meaning or interpretation or seeing things in a different light. Often, we find ourselves stuck in the rut of certain ways of thinking—our fixed mindsets—resulting in missing out on new ways of solving problems or understanding what's going on.

Here's an example of how, if we change the frame through which we interpret things, we change the meaning. The same picture below has two different frames and vastly different interpretations.

My Wife and My Mother-in-Law

Beautiful young lady, looking away from you.

Old lady with a hooked nose, looking down and sad.

If we get a knock on the door at midday, we might welcome it, possibly expecting a parcel to arrive. If the same thing happens at midnight when we're in bed, our response will probably be different and we might get alarmed. It's the same event with a different frame and therefore a different response. Much of comedy is based on reframes; a sudden new way of seeing things. For example, one of the classic comedy reframes is when the comedian Eric Morecombe responded to Andre Previn's jibe about not playing the piano properly by saying *I am playing the right notes—but not necessarily in the right order.* (In case you've not seen this wonderful clip before, you can find it on YouTube. But even if you have seen it before, treat yourself by looking at it once more . . .):

Andre Previn: Playing All the Right Notes!
A tribute from the Morecambe and Wise Christmas Show
1971 (YouTube)

A useful example of reframing is the often-uttered comment:

"In the big scheme of things, how important is this?"

This simple question has the power to significantly change a huge issue into something which is not so important because we're being invited to see it in a larger context, i.e. a different frame.

When we spot negative self talk about ourselves, such as:

- *I'm not good enough*
- *I'm a failure*
- *I feel helpless,*

we can use this technique of reframing to change such thoughts.

For example, imagine someone says to themself like:

Rainy days make me feel depressed. I hate rainy days.

Imagine thinking that every half hour or so throughout the course of a rainy day!

There are lots of possible ways to reframe such thinking, including:

Ah, good, another day for staying inside all day, all snug and safe and able to do one of my passions which is my craft work.

or . . .

Another chance to get all dressed up and warm and go for a walk in the park.

Let's say someone we know has a habit of running down other people we care about. How might we reframe how we think about this person and the situation? We might for example use one of the following frames to help us think about this person in a more compassionate way:

- *he's feeling ill*
- *he didn't get a good night's sleep*
- *he's stressed about something*
- *other people treat him in the same way*
- *I wonder if he had a rotten start in life?*

A key skill in living a happy and productive life is the ability to be aware of the frames we use to make sense of the world around us and, if appropriate, to make better choices of these frames.

We conclude this chapter with an insight on the importance of us each *actively choosing our attitudes* from Viktor Frankl. From the 1930s, he was working as a prominent Viennese psychiatrist before being incarcerated in Auschwitz for the duration of World War 2. He used his awful experiences there to write his ground breaking book *Man's Search for Meaning*, in which he says:

> **"Everything can be taken from a person, but one thing—the last of the human freedoms which is to choose one's attitude in any situation. To choose one's own way."**

In other words, when all else is lost, we each ultimately retain the human freedom to choose our attitudes—to ourselves to others and to the world.

In Summary

In this chapter, we've explored issues around our attitudes and beliefs. In particular, we've looked at:

- how our attitudes and beliefs shape how we perceive the world
- the deep seated mindsets we all carry around with us and how these can shape the quality of our lives
- 5 tips on actions we can take to shift any unhelpful attitudes or beliefs, all of which involve small, repeated actions which, once taken, can become established as useful and positive habits, producing more happiness.

We hope this may have prompted some thoughts, questions or even possible actions in your mind. And we would now gently encourage you to pause and jot these down before we move onto the next chapter which is all about the topic of our habits concerning *Appreciation*.

Of course, it could be that now, you may be tempted to invest in a tiny notebook and begin to use this as a daily or weekly journal?

CHAPTER 6
APPRECIATION

The term *appreciation* indicates a mindset or attitude where someone values something or somebody; another term for this is gratitude. Research by people such as Martin Seligman in the field of positive psychology clearly shows a strong link between our happiness as individuals and as a society and the degree to which we instinctively think and express gratitude. Closely allied to gratitude is the concept of compassion, which also involves a positive, appreciative mindset. From early childhood, we develop underlying mindsets (or habits of thinking) towards ourselves, others and the world, which may or may not tend towards gratitude or compassion.

So, clearly, our habits in these 2 related areas are worthy of exploring here. In this chapter, we start with gratitude.

THE NEUROSCIENCE OF GRATITUDE

If you knew of a way to cheer up someone else and at the same time improve your own happiness and health, we're pretty sure you'd want to do it. The good news is that recent research on the brain clearly shows that when we express gratitude, tiny changes happen to the structure of our brains to make us happier and healthier.

People who practice gratitude experience fewer aches and pains, sleep better, have higher rates of resilience, increased self esteem, immunity, happiness, energy, optimism and empathy. For example, researchers in the American based Greater Good Science Centre used fMRI brain scans to examine the brain structures of people who had been over time developing stronger habits of gratitude. They found that the part of these people's brains which is responsible for generating positive emotions (the medial prefrontal cortex) had become more sensitive and responsive. A useful place to find out more about the details on this is:

positivepsychology.com/neuroscience-of-gratitude/

From the research available, we know when we express and receive gratitude, our brain releases dopamine and serotonin, the two crucial neurotransmitters responsible for our emotions. They enhance our mood immediately, making us feel happy from the inside. By consciously practicing gratitude every day, we can help these neural pathways to strengthen themselves and ultimately create a permanent grateful and positive nature within ourselves. The effect of gratitude on the brain is long lasting (Moll, Zahn, et al. 2007). Besides enhancing self-love and empathy, gratitude significantly impacts on body functions and psychological conditions like stress, anxiety and depression. Gratitude gets rid of toxic emotions in our bodies.

The reasons why gratitude is impactful to health and wellbeing begin in the brain. In a neurological experiment conducted by researchers at the University of California in Los Angeles, brain activity was measured using magnetic resonance imaging as subjects were induced to feel gratitude by receiving gifts. The following diagram shows the location of the prefrontal cortex (just behind the forehead) which has been shown to become more sensitive through repeated actions of gratitude.

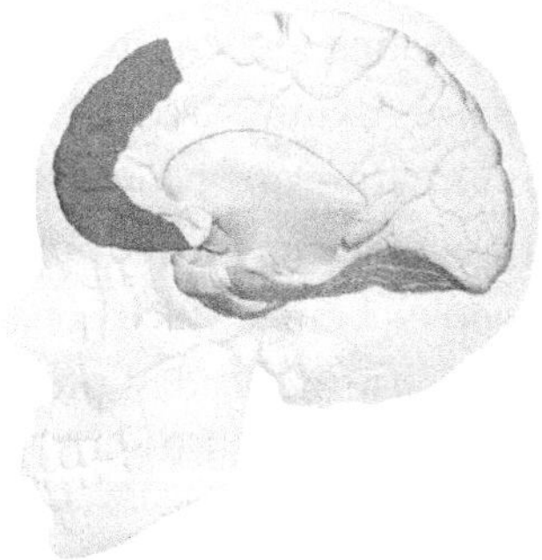

A study called *Counting Blessings vs Burdens* (2003) evaluated the effect of gratitude on physical wellbeing. It concluded that 16% of the participants who kept a gratitude journal reported better physical health. Another research study (Zahn et al., 2009) revealed that showing gratitude improves sleep quality. This study showed that a brain filled with gratitude and kindness is more likely to sleep better and wake up feeling refreshed and energetic every morning.

Finally, we also know that gratitude helps us manage our stress and anxiety levels. Research by McCraty (1998) found that participants who felt grateful showed a marked reduction in the level of cortisol, the stress hormone. They had improved cardiac functioning and were more resilient to emotional setbacks and negative experiences. Studies over the years have established that by practicing gratitude, we can handle stress better. By merely acknowledging and appreciating the little things in life, we can rewire the brain to deal with the present circumstances with more awareness and broader perception.

All well and good, but how, in the real world, can we go about this? Below are 3 ideas:

1. **Each day, (or night), reflect on any good thing that's happened over the past day.** This can be as simple as enjoying a decent cup of coffee, reading a joke or finding a car parking space on a busy Friday morning.
2. **Write gratitude letters.** A gratitude letter is written to someone in your life to express appreciation for ways they have helped you and/or been there for you. In June 2017, researchers Joshua Brown and Joel Wong conducted experiments to assess the benefits of gratitude letters. They found that the act of focussing on the positives and away from toxic thoughts significantly enhanced the wellbeing of those who wrote gratitude letters. Participants in the experiments, though, weren't required to send their letters to their intended recipient. In fact, only 23% of participants sent them. Those who didn't send their letters enjoyed the same increases in

wellbeing as those who did send them. There is still a significant increase in the release of the happiness chemicals dopamine and serotonin and a rewiring of our brains just by the act of expressing gratitude to ourselves and/or by the simple act of writing it down.

3. **Make a gratitude list**. A gratitude list involves writing down 3 to 5 things for which we're grateful every day, each week, at other intervals, or under situation specific circumstances. Again, the mere act of writing down a list of things we're grateful for releases the *feel good* hormones of dopamine and serotonin, resulting in us feeling happier.

Research by the John Templeton Foundation has found that in the US, there's a large gap between the gratitude people feel and the expression of that gratitude. According to the study, 90% of Americans say they feel grateful for their families, yet only 52% of women and 44% of men express their gratitude on a regular basis. Given the benefit in overall happiness when people express gratitude, it's worth asking whether many of us are missing out on possible big increases in happiness.

Another useful challenge to work on is to learn how to improve our skills in gracefully receiving thanks. Some of us may be more comfortable at giving thanks, rather than gracefully receiving it. For example, how many people do you know who, when you express gratitude to them for something, may *discount* it to some degree, by saying something like *it wasn't me really, it was the whole team*, or *it wasn't anything really.* Maybe we all would benefit from learning how to be more comfortable accepting appreciation and gratitude when we receive it, by saying something, like, *That's kind of you. I really appreciate your words.*

COMPASSION

This word is well used in society and there are no doubt lots of ways of defining it. First, we suggest splitting the concept into 2 parts:

- self compassion
- compassion for others.

We would define each of these in the following ways:

Self compassion

- having kind thoughts and feelings towards ourselves
- managing the negative self talk, sometimes called the *inner critic* which often unhelpfully natters away inside our heads.

Compassion for others

- appreciating how others may be thinking and feeling about things
- being able to step into their shoes and get a sense of what life's like for them
- having supporting and kind thoughts and feelings for them
- expressing these thoughts and feelings towards others in whatever way is appropriate and helpful to them.

In the real world, both these types of compassion offer their challenges (and benefits) for happiness.

Self compassion

How many of us can really say that *we always treat ourselves as we would treat a best friend*? Sadly, the opposite is often true. How many people, whether family members, work colleagues, neighbours or friends do you know who work too hard, get excessively stressed, over anxious, depressed and unfit? When it comes to compassion, the very first person we need to learn to show more compassion to, is ourselves.

A key part of this is spotting the unkind things we sometimes say to ourselves and replacing this language with more useful messages. For example, before an important event in our life, we may find our self talk, (sometimes described as our *inner critic*), whispering toxic things in our ears, like: *Typical of me . . . always late and never able to do things properly.*

When we spot such unhelpful toxic language in our ear, it pays dividends to reject it, replacing it with a new message which we can repeat such as, *Time to show me at my very best. I'm worth it and I can do it.*

> **"Self compassion is the practice of quieting your inner critic, and replacing it with a voice of support, understanding and caring for yourself."**

One of the leading researchers in the field of self compassion is Dr Kristin Neff from the University of Texas. Having self compassion, according to Dr. Neff, is not about trying to be perfect. It's about being kind and understanding, even when faced with personal failings.

Self compassion is not about self judgment either. It's about developing a sense of warmth and compassion in everything we do. When we're self compassionate, we recognize our own failures and shortcomings as things that are likely to happen from time to time and which we can accept with love and kindness.

Self compassion also allows us to see that all humans suffer.

> **"The very definition of being human means we are vulnerable, imperfect and mortal."**

Self compassion comes into play when we're able to recognize this definition of what it means to be human.

Dr Neff's work also involves the concept of mindfulness, which we explore in chapter 3.

But how do we go about embedding more compassion into our lives?

The answer is to take *a tiny step each day*. And then, after a surprisingly short time, we find that a new and positive habit has begun to develop, where we find ourselves taking more care towards our own selves.

By practising self compassion, we can turn the enemies in our head into friends.

There's no doubt that transforming your *inner critic* into an *inner coach* is a big ask, probably a lifelong ambition. The key though, as we've said, is to take tiny steps. For example, spot something you find today in your self talk, stop it in its tracks and convert it into something kind that you say to yourself about yourself. Do this every day, making it a habit and your journey will have truly started.

Dr Neff's research indicates that self compassion is associated with greater emotional resilience, better self awareness and more caring relationships, as well as less narcissism and anger:

> **"People who are compassionate to themselves are much more likely to be happy, resilient, optimistic and motivated to change themselves and their lives for the better. When**

our inner voice plays the role of a supportive friend (not a continual critic), then when we notice some personal failing, we feel safe and accepted enough to make the changes needed to be healthier and happier."

Compassion for others

Not surprisingly, our self talk can also comment on other people and the way we interpret the world around us. Unless we've found a way of saying positive things to ourselves, that voice will also say negative things about other people, such as: *She's always late . . . He's a waste of space . . . She's a nasty piece of work* or *Typical of him—he never helps out.*

If we stop and listen to ourselves and others, we can sometimes spot and (if we want to) stop the unhelpful self talk, replacing it with something more useful. Most people do the best they can, given the choices they think they have. The thing is, though, most of us actually have far more choices in how we think and behave than we believe.

Unless we're careful, this internal chatter about ourselves and others can too easily become habits of how we think, some of which may not always serve us well. By recognizing such unhelpful habits of thinking, we can take the first step towards stopping them and thinking about others in a more compassionate and helpful way.

"If you want others to be happy, practice compassion. If you want to be happy, practice compassion."

—Dalai Lama

Every encounter with a person provides us with an opportunity to show compassion for others. For example, when we're in the checkout queue in the supermarket, the staff member usually wears a name badge. The tiniest thing we can do to show more compassion is to call them by their name—a tiny but significant kind act that can make a difference to another person's day. For some reason, most of us hang back from offering feedback to others—even when it's positive. Another way to show more compassion to others is to look for genuine opportunities to say how we enjoy and appreciate certain things others do that affect us. When we turn our minds to it, there are many opportunities to be more generous (in an authentic and sensitive way) with our positive feedback to others.

During the Covid-19 pandemic, we've all been touched by many *random acts of kindness* shown all over the world, from Italian people singing from their flat balconies to Brits clapping in the street for NHS and other front-line workers. The Covid-19 period has been a true test of our inner resilience, but as the Mental Health Foundation says:

"Doing good makes us feel good."

They have more about this on their website at:

mentalhealth.org.uk/publications/
doing-good-does-you-good

In chapter 9 called *Action*, we return more fully to the theme of Random Acts of Kindness.

As we move to the conclusion of this chapter on the habits of *Appreciation*, it's important to clarify that there is no necessary link between having well embedded habits of gratitude and compassion and being excessively over optimistic, like the character Pollyanna. (*Pollyanna* was the title of a novel written for children in 1913 by Eleanor Porter which featured a character of the same name who was very exuberant and over optimistic).

The person with well embedded habits of gratitude and compassion will also be able to disagree with others, if necessary and to deliver quality, constructive feedback to help others on their journey. As Mahatma Gandhi once said:

> **"Honest disagreement is often a good sign of progress."**

In Summary

In this chapter, we've explored issues around our habits regarding *Appreciation*, in particular:

- the role that feeling and expressing gratitude plays in our happiness
- the role that compassion—for self for others and for the world plays in our happiness.

As with other parts of the book, we trust this may have prompted some thoughts, questions and actions; and we would invite you to pause and make a note of these before we move onto the next chapter, which is all about our habits regarding setting and acting on our *Aims* in life.

CHAPTER 7
AIMS

When we hear people talking about their lives, a metaphor we may sometimes hear them use is that *life's a journey*. But as we know, that *journey* can often be a long and difficult road, particularly when we're bombarded with TV programmes, adverts and social media, inviting us to buy this, buy that, do this or do that.

When we're in our car, if we're setting out on a long and new journey, what's the thing that most of us habitually do, before we get started out on the road? Probably, to pull up our sat nav, input the destination postcode and begin to follow the instructions provided.

But how many of us have got well established habits which help us navigate the journey of life? Many of us travel on life's journey with no clear sense of direction at all. This is why Stephen Covey is so right to place so much importance on *Putting First Things First*:

"Putting first things first means organizing and executing around your most important priorities. It is living and being driven by the principles you value most, not by the agendas and forces surrounding you."

Years ago, when life was simpler, maybe it didn't matter so much, but in a society where we're bombarded with advertising (which for the most part is cleverly designed to tempt and influence us to do some things we wouldn't otherwise consider, particularly how we spend our money and our time), it's more valuable than ever to know, deep down, what's most important in our lives.

An organisation called OpenDemocracy (www.open domocracy.net) has calculated that what we mostly see on TV, in terms of sheer volume, is not comedy, drama or sport, but *advertising*. They calculate that the average British viewer is now exposed to 48 TV commercials a day. Recent studies showed that around 33% of Australian TV time is now taken up by commercials. In the US the figures are closer to 40%. Against this background, it can be easy to lose sight of what's most important in life and to lose focus on the things that make us most happy.

How do we do this?

There are two tools which can help us here:

- clarifying the factors that are most important in our lives
- setting personal goals which provide a clear sense of direction for our lives.

Research by Damon Burton in 1983 has shown that people who do these things effectively:

- enjoy a clear and focused direction giving a sense of security and purpose
- use their time well
- have good self-esteem, confidence and belief in their ability to make things happen and feel in control
- are happier and more satisfied.

This is why in this chapter, we focus on:

- a simple and effective way to help us surface the factors that are most important to us
- tools to help us clarify our aims in life and turn these into goals and outcomes.

CLARIFYING WHAT'S MOST IMPORTANT TO US

Many of us have never had the encouragement and support to help us understand what's most important to us in life. It's either assumed we all know or that it's not important to know.

If we've never paused to define what's most important to us, it's like sailing on the ocean without a compass. We're leaving ourselves vulnerable to the next trend, fashion or meme.

What follows next is a short and powerful exercise to help clarify the factors that are most important to us in life. Some people would call these values.

The exercise consists of *4 stages*.

Exercise: What's most important to me?

Step 1

Scan the list of factors below and circle up to a ***maximum of 10 factors*** which for you are the most important:

Achievement
Adaptability
Ambition
Being liked
Being the best
Caring
Caution
Challenge
Compassion
Competence
Contribution to society
Control
Courage
Creativity
Dependability
Details
Efficiency
Enthusiasm
Environmental awareness
Ethics
Excellence

Friendship
Generosity
Happiness
Health
Humour
Integrity
Job security
Learning
Listening
Making a difference
Money
Power
Recognition
Relationships
Reliability
Respect
Reward
Risk taking
Safety
Self reliance
Trust

Fairness
Family
Financial stability
Forgiveness
Use of my talents
Well being
Wisdom
Vision

Step 2

Write the factors you circled, into the table below:

Factors That Matter Most to Me

Step 3

Reflect on which of the above factors are most important for you in life today and/or in the next 12 months or so. Write these in the table below. Try to keep the number you identify here, to a maximum of 3 factors. (If you're able to put these into priority order, please do so).

Factors That Matter Most to Me

For each of the above factors, reflect on how well you're doing.

For example, if one of your top factors is work/life balance and you're finding yourself away at work for 60 hours per week or more, you may well consider that you should be doing better on this factor.

One useful way to self assess yourself is to use a scale of 1–10, where a score of 10 is your ideal and a score of 1 is very poor.

Then, ask yourself questions such as:

- what am I already doing well on this factor and possibly could do more of, to increase my score?
- what do I need to do less of, or stop doing, to increase my score?
- what new actions do I need to do to move closer to my ideal score of 10?

Step 4

Add in your scores for each factor, into the following table:

My Most Important Factors	Self Score (1–10)

This exercise gives us a sense of where we are and where we need to change direction. Both of which are important factors when we're on a journey.

In a sense, this is *our map and our compass* which we now need to use as we move onto setting our aims, converting these into goals and reviewing our progress in meeting them.

TURNING AIMS INTO GOALS AND GOALS INTO OUTCOMES

For the moment, let's go *BIG.* And we mean **HUGE**.

Dare to dream of the things you want most from life. For example, you might want to be fit, healthy, slim and toned. That's fine. You may want to finesse this slightly. After all, to get a streamlined body at the age of 60 may be wonderful but if your image is of someone who's 25 years old and can spend three hours in the gym, several times a week, you may end up creating your own passage to downfall. How about if we made this goal to be as general as *To be at optimum fitness, health and weight for my age.* Does that sound more achievable and less threatening?

Stage 1: create some huge goals

A Stage 1 goal might be something like, *to be at optimum fitness for someone of my age.*

Now, we need to make this more specific, realistic and achievable by breaking this goal down into more bitesize chunks.

Stage 2: make them realistic for you at your time of life and yet still ensure they're worthy of your dreams and motivate you to want to achieve.

Stage 3: break all this down into what it'll mean when you've achieved these goals. What will you see, hear and feel?

It might be that your Body Mass Index (BMI) is in the healthy range between 18.5 and 24.9 and you'll know this when you calculate your BMI on your monthly checks. You might find yourself *jogging up* that hill which once made you puff and pant like a steam train.

Finally, you might see an image of yourself, playing with young members of your family, chasing, catching or kicking a ball, clambering into their den and not ending up with a cricked neck, a pulled muscle or painful back when you wake the following morning.

You might by now have a list which looks like this:

HUGE GOAL	To be fit, healthy and slim.
REALISTIC GOAL	To be at optimum weight and fitness for my age and motivation.
EVIDENCE	1. To have a BMI between 22.9 and 23.5. 2. To run the June 5K race for life. 3. To take the family to Alton Towers and go on the best rides. 4. To get out of bed every morning without groaning. 5. To touch my toes again.
ACTIONS	

So far, the final column (headed ACTIONS) has been left empty. This is where we get serious about committing to a small step with an end date. So what's the smallest step to be taken on the road to achieving this goal?

The goal must be small. If it's too large, it may not happen and the sense of failure can be overwhelming. Make it small enough and possible and success is more likely. Nothing is guaranteed, as humans are strange creatures and all sorts of things can scupper our attempts to develop or change our unhelpful habits into more helpful ones.

A good example of this approach can be found on the NHS website:

www.nhs.uk/live-well/exercise/
couch-to-5k-week-by-week/

This programme provides a step by step programme to help people progress *from the couch* to completing a 5k run in 9 weeks. Week 1 begins with a brisk 5 mins walk, after which the programme includes a range of other activities, each of which subtly builds on the previous stages. The impact of this 9 week running plan has now been tried and tested on thousands of new runners and it's been proved to work well. Interestingly, the programme also makes it clear that an important part of the programme is a number of rest days.

A really good example of *turning tiny steps into giant strides.*

**"One tiny step at a time. . . .
Turning tiny steps into giant strides."**

Here's a common mistake a lot of people make, *too much, too soon.* You might want amazing abs but starting with a small number of crunches, sit ups and time spent on the plank and increasing by one every few days will build up slowly and surely.

Populating the table we have already created with some small achievable actions might end up something like this.

HUGE GOAL	To be fit, healthy and slim.
REALISTIC GOAL	To be at optimum weight and fitness for my age and motivation.
EVIDENCE	1. To have a BMI between 22.9 and 23.5. 2. To run the June 5K race for life. 3. To take the family to Alton Towers and go on the best rides. 4. To get out of bed every morning without groaning. 5. To touch my toes again.
ACTIONS	**To touch my toes again.** *Day 1:* check how far down I can stretch and do two. *Day 2:* repeat and increase one per day until I can do ten. *Day 13:* check online for tips on improving my suppleness. *Day 14:* check how far I can now stretch down and repeat the process outlined above.

By structuring your goals in this way, they become achievable rather than plunging you into despair when you don't reach them. However, if you find yourself not motivated and can't be bothered, are these really the goals for you?

One challenge we all have to face is reality versus the advertising and Instagram version of reality which swamps the viewer with images of perfection and happiness. Not true. If we were to gather together the images of happiness from these sources, they might include some of the following, in no specific order:

- perfect teeth
- driving a new, shiny car on a beach, a mountain highway or in a deserted city
- surrounded by family and friends

- everyone laughs and smiles all the time
- perfect bodies
- a dog (or a cat)
- a huge kitchen with friends or family grouped round for an evening meal and no messy saucepans in the sink
- spreads of food that would feed thousands (especially true in the run up to Christmas)
- alcohol—lots of it and no hangovers.

There's plenty more. But is this the life that we really, *deeply* want? These things may lift us for a while, but all will probably have their natural shelf life. And the one message that we're so often encouraged to take on board is this; buy my product and you'll be happier, more attractive, more successful, richer, more popular etc.

Is it true? Of course, not. These messages can seep subliminally into our conscious and unconscious minds and if our lives are not up to these imagined and created standards, is it no wonder we feel more dissatisfied with our lot and as a result less happy?

This is why the goals we create for ourselves must mean something and be motivating to us.

In Summary

We've now covered the various ways we might deal with how we set aims and act on them, hopefully making them good habits for life. In particular, we've explored:

- the importance of understanding what's most important, (deep down) to us—an exercise which gives us a *compass* we can then use to help us navigate our way through life
- how to turn aims into goals; and how to turn goals into outcomes.

Now is the time to pause and capture any thoughts, questions or actions on paper as we next move onto our habits of *Adventure*!

CHAPTER 8

ADVENTURE

In the last chapter, we referred to the metaphor people sometimes use when they're talking about their life, i.e. that life is *a journey*. We were reminded of this recently when we were with friends looking back at photos of our younger selves. One of them remarked *how far we've all come* . . . And it's true.

Another powerful metaphor often used to describe life is that it's a *quest;* a term Viktor Frankl (whom we introduced in chapter 5 on *Attitudes*), used in his book *Man's Search for Meaning.*

So, what does it mean to live life as a quest? We suggest that such a deep down attitude to life involves:

- learning and developing
- extending our comfort zones
- moving on.

And that's where we're going next. How do we live life?

First, let's consider the approach to life of one of the UK's most recent public heroes, the late Captain Sir Tom Moore, who at the age of 99, began to walk laps of his garden in aid of charity with the goal of raising £1,000 by his hundredth birthday.

When asked how he saw life, Captain Tom used to say:

> **"Today will be a good day. Tomorrow, you will maybe find everything will be much better than today, even if today was all right. My today was all right and my tomorrow will certainly be better. That's the way I've always looked at life."**
>
> **—Captain Sir Tom Moore, April 2020**

We can clearly see in this quote that, deep down, Captain Tom saw life as a quest and an adventure in which he always sought to extend his comfort zone, move on, learn and develop.

In chapter 5, we explored the well-researched area of optimism, drawing on the work of Martin Seligman in his book *Learned Optimism* and we touched on the benefits of optimism. This doesn't mean there's no place for pessimism. If we see life as an adventure, it surely makes sense to assess risks and plan for them within the adventure. To have a successful and happy life, we need to use both mindsets (optimism and pessimism) wisely and to get a good balance, thus making ourselves more resilient:

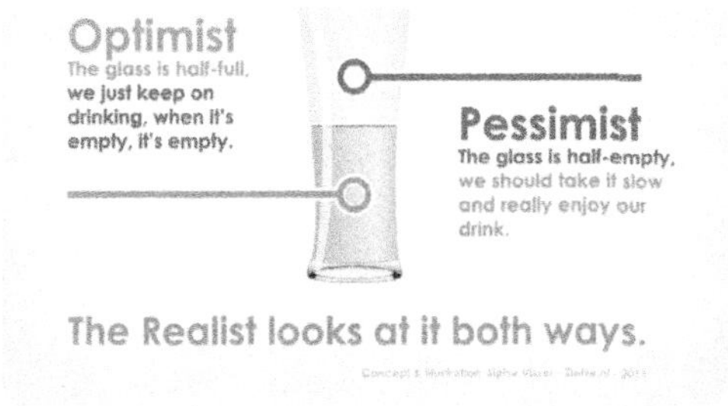

Regardless of which mindset is our preference in life, we all have at least one thing in common, which is that our brains have created strong, well embedded habits of thinking, regardless of whether they tend towards optimism or pessimism.

One of these habits is the creation of a *comfort zone*; a way of thinking and behaving which is safe, comfortable and automatic.

In 2006, researchers Ryan and Markova developed a valuable model to help us understand better what tends to go on for us when we step outside our comfort zone and deal with life outside it. The model is often shown as below:

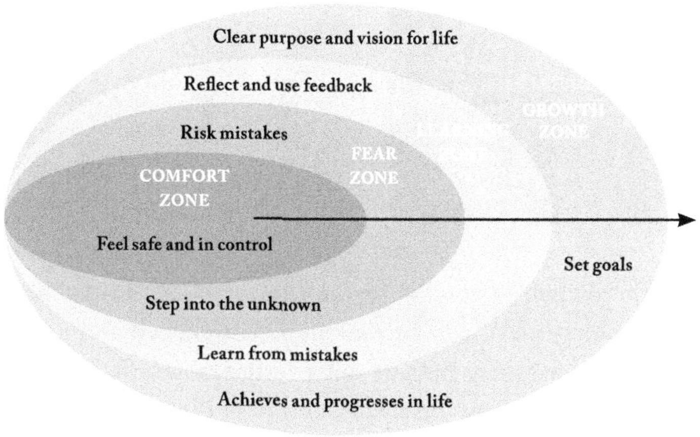

COMFORT ZONE

In the comfort zone, we live life automatically. We follow patterns. We brush our teeth without thinking about how to do it. We may tend to keep the same hairstyle, the same style of clothing, or watch the same TV programmes. The comfort zone is just that, comfortable.

We all need to spend time in our comfort zone to nourish ourselves, restore our nervous system and gather our strength for the next challenge. The comfort zone isn't bad; it's just not the place where new growth occurs.

In the comfort zone, we may experience:

- a sense of calm and being at ease
- comfort
- safety
- a place for gathering our strength
- a place of recovery
- low levels of anxiety
- possibly, (after a while) boredom.

The danger of staying in the comfort zone for too long is that our patterns can become more entrenched and unless we occasionally step outside our comfort zone, we can stop learning and miss out on the adventure of life.

FEAR ZONE

In order to live life to the full, we all need from time to time to leave the comfort zone and do something new. Sometimes, this can bring with it a degree of discomfort, unease or even fear.

It can be something as simple as driving to a new town we've not been to before and being uncertain of the route or the one way system or where to park. Or it can be something like starting a new job, or moving to a new part of the country. In such circumstances, we can feel uncomfortable. When we start doing new things, it can be unsettling. When we're doing something new, it's more likely that we may make mistakes or even fail.

Unless we're sufficiently self confident, it's tempting to stay in the comfort zone and avoid the risk of failure. On the other hand, we could take the view:

Nothing ventured, nothing gained.

The fear zone is a place we need to visit quite frequently in life—a place where we can sometimes make mistakes if need be, try new things out and get some new learnings under our belt. One approach is to take *small steps* into the fear zone repeatedly, until we look back and see the tiny steps have eventually turned into giant strides.

Have you ever learnt a new skill such as playing the piano, playing golf or learning to cook a new dish? There may have been times when you were apprehensive and made mistakes, but it's the learnings from such experiences that free you up to move to the next zone, which is the learning zone.

LEARNING ZONE

Once we've been brave enough to venture outside the comfort zone and experience new things, we're ready to move into the learning zone. It's a place to rethink our current patterns, challenging ourselves, taking risks with our thinking and actions and feeling more alive than we do now. We need to be in this zone to learn and grow. But we can't remain in this zone all the time, or we'll burn out. We need to know when it's time to retreat to the comfort zone, to rest, reflect and consolidate our learnings.

Some of the qualities we may experience in the learning zone are:

- engaging with the new or unknown
- taking manageable risks
- challenging ourselves but not too much
- being excited, energized, engaged, motivated but not overwhelmed
- learning, growth and success.

One way some people make the best from their learnings and their movements from zone to zone is to keep a journal, where they keep track of their experiences, their challenges and any mistakes and learnings.

GROWTH ZONE

As we reflect on our experiences, we can build new confidence and knowledge into our expanded comfort zone and move on in life, setting new goals and ambitions, thus moving into our growth zone. This is an area where we consciously reach out and set the huge life goals we talked about in chapter 7 (*Aims*), chunking them down into repeated tiny steps, with a confident sense of knowing what's most important to us.

Karl Rohnke, (a key figure in the development of adventure education in the 1970s), developed the zone model based on the Yerke's-Dodson Law, which says that peak performance occurs when people experience a moderate level of pressure. When there's too much or too little pressure, performance declines. To be at our best, we each need to operate under the right amount of pressure which *uniquely* suits us best.

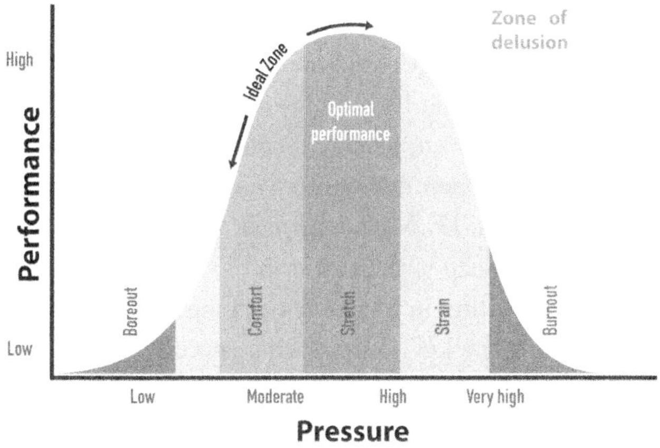

GET TO KNOW YOUR ZONES

For some people, tiny steps each taken with great care, accompanied by time to recover in the comfort zone, is how they perform best. For others, bigger challenges are needed to help them be at their best. Each person is different and that's why we each need to know ourselves well to get the best out of our life.

When we're in the growth zone, we know ourselves well enough to understand exactly how we need to recharge our batteries and what kind of challenges we need to perform at our best. At this point, we really are in the driving seat for our happiness.

If we want to change and grow in any area of our lives—health, fitness, career, personal development, spiritual growth, among others—we need to know where our own zones begin and end and how to optimize them.

However, if we don't know ourselves well enough and don't have clear boundaries, someone else may push us too soon into the fear zone. Think of the demanding boss, the parent with high expectations, or the spouse that puts pressure on us. Self knowledge and knowing our boundaries are an integral part of leading a happy and fulfilled life.

Part of the challenge of how to get the best out of ourselves includes knowing what time of day we do our best work. This will vary from person to person of course, but there's growing awareness about when our brains work best in the day and when to rest them. Dr Michael Breus, who specialises in the neuroscience of sleep is the author of *The Power of When.* He believes that working in harmony with our body's and brain's natural clock is the key to unlocking success to produce our best, most creative work and it's at these times when it's best to move out of the comfort zone. Michael Breus says:

> **"An inner clock embedded inside your brain has been ticking away, keeping perfect time, since you were a baby. This precisely engineered timekeeper is called your circadian pacemaker, or biological clock."**

For some people, learning is most effective when the brain is in so called *acquisition* mode, generally between 10:00 am to 2:00 pm and then again from 4:00 pm to 10:00 pm. The phrase *sleep on it* has persisted for a reason; most of us tend to make worse decisions late at night and first thing in the morning. Our cognitive powers are strongest once our brain has had a chance to shake off its sleep inertia.

Dr Breus' research has found that some people are at their least creative when it's often demanded the most, at the heart of the workday, between 11:00 am to 3:00 pm.

This research is in its infancy and so the most important thing is to notice for yourself what times in the day (or night) your energy and brain are at their best and most productive and use this information to create your habits of work and life. For example, if we have a challenging piece of work to do and if we're at our best first thing in the morning, perhaps we should make sure we do this work first thing in the day.

Take some time to get to know your own zones. Here are some questions to reflect upon or journal:

- how much time, roughly speaking, do you spend in each zone each week? How does that feel to you?
- what does your comfort zone look like in different areas (work, home, social relations, health, etc)?
- how does your body feel when you're in the comfort zone?
- what signs tell you it's time to return to your comfort zone? Do you listen to them?
- do you spend too much time in your comfort zone, not enough, or the right amount?
- what internal voices do you hear when you attempt to move out of your comfort zone into your fear or learning zones?
- what is something new and different you would like to do or learn?
- what does your body feel like when you're in your fear or learning zone?
- how do you know you're in your fear zone?
- what tools, resources, or personal messages help you move from your fear zone to your comfort zone?

Answering some or all of these questions may provide you with valuable information on your working preferences but there's another important habit we need to focus on next, which is *sleep*.

SLEEP

Thomas Dekker, the 17th century dramatist, once said:

> **"Sleep is the golden chain that binds health and our bodies together."**

Brain science tells us that we should spend about a third of our lives asleep. Sleep is essential—it's as important to our bodies as eating, drinking and breathing and is vital for maintaining good mental and physical health. Sleeping helps us to recover from mental as well as physical exertion.

Sleep and health are strongly related. Poor sleep can increase the risk of having poor health and poor health can make it harder to sleep. Sleep disturbances can be one of the first signs of distress. Common mental health problems like anxiety and depression can often underpin sleep problems.

In order to feel fully rested again and to achieve *optimal alertness* throughout the day, there's one long-term solution that never fails—we must repay our *sleep debt* hour for hour.

A helpful way to understand sleep debt is to think of personal energy as a bank. You deposit energy into your account when you're asleep and you make withdrawals when you're awake. If you're spending too much time awake and not enough time sleeping, then your energy bank balance is in deficit; you have a sleep debt.

Far and away the most important aspect of the regulation of sleep is this simple fact; *sleep loss is cumulative*. When total nightly sleep is reduced by exactly the same amount each night for several consecutive nights, the tendency to fall asleep in the daytime becomes progressively stronger each day and performance is often compromised as a result.

The NHS calculates that most adults need around 8 hours of quality sleep a night. Data from America (www.terrycralle.com) tells us that in 2019, 52% of children didn't get enough sleep and that 33% of adults were in sleep debt.

Sleep debt has the potential to create many problems:

Sleep debt decreases alertness and ability to maintain focus

Carrying a sizeable sleep debt throughout the day can drastically decrease productivity. Fatigue will compromise our attention and as a result cognitive performance will suffer. Specifically, learning, memory and creativity are frequently hampered by a large sleep debt. In a situation such as driving a car. This decreased alertness can and has repeatedly led to fatal results.

Sleep debt destabilises our mood

It's not uncommon for sleep deprived individuals to be subject to extreme emotions and mood swings. A very tired person who's laughing uncontrollably one moment may be crying or yelling angrily a few minutes later. Writing in *Psychology Today* in 2021, Dr Michael Breus describes how sleep deprivation increases activity in the *amygdala* (part of the *mammal brain* we talked about in chapter 2). This part of the brain controls many of our immediate emotional reactions. When short on sleep, the amygdala goes into overdrive, causing us to be more intensely reactive to situations. Interestingly, it's not only our negative emotions, like anger and fear that get a heightened response. Studies show that, when sleep deprived, we're more reactive across the whole spectrum of emotions, positive and negative.

At the same time the amygdala is fired up, lack of sleep also hampers the communication between the amygdala and the prefrontal cortex, (part of the *human brain* which we also described in chapter 2). This area of the brain is involved in emotional regulation, a key component of our emotional intelligence. The prefrontal cortex handles complex tasks, one of which is to put the brakes on impulsiveness.

Sleep debt decreases our energy and motivation

A decrease in energy and motivation is probably the most noticeable consequence of sleep deprivation. Individuals who have not received sufficient sleep will feel lethargic and uninspired to work.

Sleep debt can adversely effect overall health and wellbeing

The NHS are clear that sleeping less than an average of about 8 hours per night can lead to conditions such as obesity. It's believed to be because sleep deprived people have reduced levels of peptin (the chemical that makes us feel full) and increased levels of ghrelin (the hunger stimulating hormone), resulting in us eating more and feeling less satisfied. Other conditions that can be triggered by sleep dept include heart disease and diabetes.

With the tendency for people to be attached to their mobile phones, tablets and other devices, as well as the TV, there's now research (by Monique LeBourgeois in the journal *Paediatrics,* November 2017) which shows the effect this is having on people's sleep habits and overall wellbeing. This research found adverse associations between screen time and sleep health—primarily because of later bedtimes and less time spent sleeping, psychological stimulation from content consumed and the negative impact of screen light on sleep patterns.

The NHS has some helpful recommendations to promote effective sleep habits. They are:

Sleep at regular times

This programmes the brain and internal body clock to get used to a set routine. Most adults need between 6 and 9 hours of sleep every night. By working out what time you need to wake up, you can set a regular bedtime schedule. It's also important to wake up at roughly the same time every day. While it may seem like a good idea to try to catch up on sleep after a bad night, doing so on a regular basis can also disrupt sleep routines.

Make sure you wind down

Winding down is a critical stage in preparing for bed. This can be done by:

- taking a warm bath (not hot) to help your body reach a temperature that's ideal for rest
- writing *to do* lists for the next day can organise thoughts and clear the mind of any distractions
- doing relaxation exercises, (such as the light stretching you might do in yoga) help us to relax the muscles (Vigorous exercise, however, will have the opposite effect)
- listening to relaxation scripts or gentle hypnotic music and sound effects
- reading a book or listening to the radio relaxes the mind by distracting it
- avoid using smartphones, tablets or other electronic devices for an hour or so before you go to bed as the light from the screen on these devices may have a negative effect on sleep.

If you'd like more information on how your sleep habits can improve, there's a free online quiz at:

psychcentral.com/quizzes/sleep-quiz/

Finally, what we conclude from all this is . . .

. . . without good quality and quantity sleep, our chances of living a happy and fulfilled life are low, if not impossible.

In Summary

In this chapter, we've explored the importance of:

- having a positive mindset where we look out for opportunities to learn from our experiences, whatever they are
- stepping out of our comfort zones and into a zone where we create new habits and patterns and thus increase the size of our comfort zone
- developing good sleeping habits, without which we're unlikely to achieve the happy and fulfilled lives we seek.

Now is a great time to capture any thoughts, feelings or actions on any of this, before we move onto the next factor, which is *Action* . . .

CHAPTER 9
ACTION

Have you noticed that some people seem to be happier than others? Some people seem more naturally inclined to happiness, but sadly, some other people struggle more with it.

Research by Sonja Lyubomirsky (2007) clearly shows that a major contributor to our personal happiness is the genes we were born with. However, the other 2 factors which contribute most to our happiness are:

- our actions and thoughts
- external circumstances.

So, at least 40% of our happiness is driven by our actions and thoughts, with an additional 10% shaped by our external circumstances.

What Determines Happiness

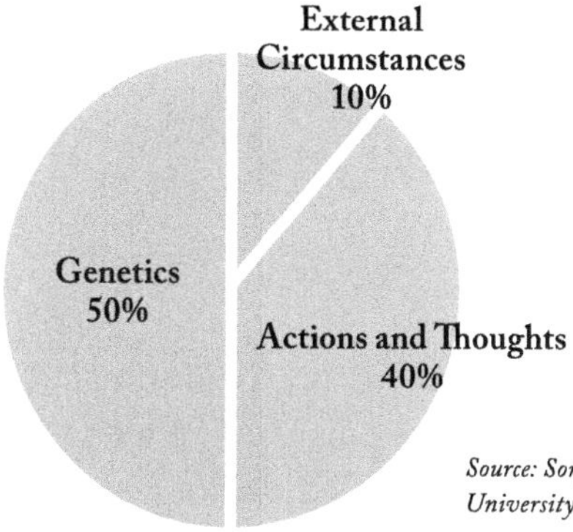

Source: Sonja Lyubomirsky, Ph. D.
University of California, Riverside

There are lots of other ways we can each take actions which impact on our personal happiness and the happiness of others. And we hope that as a result of reading this book so far, you have taken the opportunity to commit to a number of actions already.

In the following section, we highlight 3 additional ways we can choose to take action, all of which can, once repeated for a short while, become habits well embedded into our lives.

Action taking 1: making small changes into new positive habits

Every day, we have choices; to carry on thinking and doing as we've always done, to make big plans for change or to make small changes in how we think and what we do. In the end, it's often the small things that we do that tend to make most difference:

In chapter 1, we focussed on the Action for Happiness movement. One of the most popular tools they provide for free is a monthly calendar, on which there's a suggestion of a small but significant action one might aim to take on each day. This is an excellent way to create a new habit of taking small but important actions towards happiness. Their monthly calendar is available from:

www.actionforhappiness.org

Here is their March 2021 calendar:

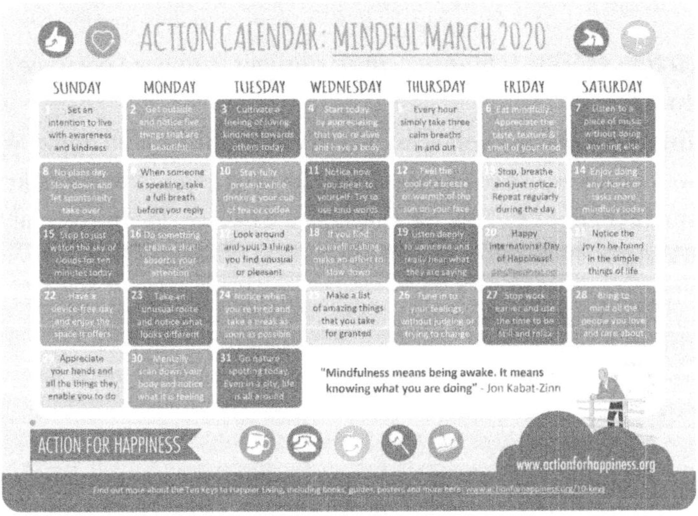

Plus, here are some other suggestions to experiment with:

- decide today to show more appreciation to someone for what they've done for you or others
- when you see someone's name badge at the checkout in the supermarket, include their name in your goodbye and thanks to them
- as you lie in bed, maybe before you drift off to sleep, or in any waking moment in the night, reflect on the day just gone and express a nice positive thought about the things that went well that day
- take time to focus on the things in life you're most grateful for
- start a journal which includes a focus on the good things in your life.

Whatever small action you commit to, you can be delighted to notice how, once you do this small action repeatedly for a period such as 2–3 months, it simply becomes a normal, automatic behaviour requiring no effort on your part. And then, you can choose to take another small action and make this, too, a habit.

Action taking 2: random acts of kindness

During the various Covid-19 social restrictions, we've all been touched by many *random acts of kindness* shown all over the world, from Italian people singing from their flat balconies to British people clapping in the street for the NHS and other front-line workers. The Covid-19 period has been a true test of our inner resilience, but as the Mental Health Foundation says:

"Doing good makes us feel good."

They have more on this on their website at:

mentalhealth.org.uk/publications/
doing-good-does-you-good

There is a solid body of science which supports the idea that random acts of kindness do good to others and ourselves. The warm feeling of wellbeing that washes over us when we've done something kind isn't just in our heads. It's in our brain and body's chemicals, too.

Acts of kindness release hormones that contribute to our mood and overall wellbeing, primarily oxytocin and serotonin. Oxytocin is sometimes called *the love hormone* in recognition of the role it plays in forming social bonds and trusting other people. It's the hormone mothers produce when they breastfeed, cementing the bond with their babies. Oxytocin is also released when we're physically intimate and when we're being kind and loving. It's tied to making us more trusting, more generous and friendlier, while also lowering our blood pressure.

Serotonin is another hormone which is boosted when we're kind. This hormone is sometimes called *the natural feel good* hormone for its key role in helping us to regulate our moods.

Acts of kindness release these valuable hormones inside us, quite apart from the benefit that the act of kindness gives to others. However, the effect isn't lasting. A single act of kindness isn't going to carry us through several days—or even hours. We need to embed them in our daily lives as a habit. The more we do this, the greater the benefit to ourselves, others and society more generally.

Kindness is Chemical

oxytocin: the love hormone
serotonin: the feel-good hormone
They are released when we're kind and loving.

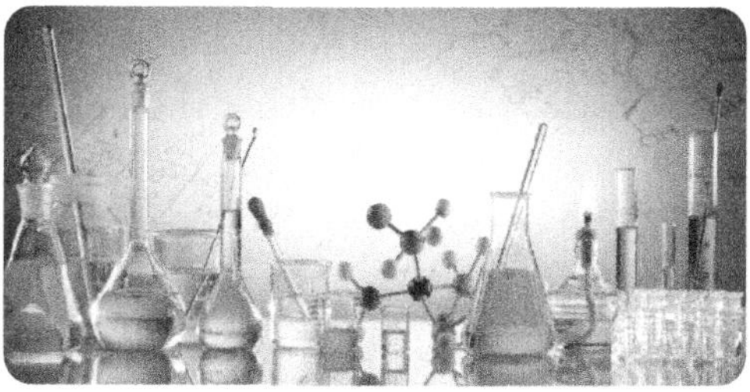

There's a long list of possible random acts of kindness we could easily choose to do, including:

- calling a friend we haven't spoken to for a while
- telling a family member how much we love and appreciate them
- arranging to have a cup of tea and virtual catch up with someone we know
- telling someone we know that we're proud of them
- giving up our place in the supermarket queue for someone who has only a few items
- calling out *thank you* when the post comes through the door.

The list is endless . . .

As Dr Stephen Post's research (2007) shows:

> **"A candle loses nothing of its light by lighting another candle. By lighting the heart of someone else, we allow out own hearts to be lit."**

It's good to know that Stephen Post is not alone in this thinking. A dynamic and innovative organisation in America, called *Kindness* believes that kindness is the catalyst for solving the world's greatest challenges. They are a non-profit organisation, grounded in research, with the mission to educate and inspire people to choose kindness. They encourage people, organisations and communities to do acts of kindness. In so doing, they promote the concept that the accumulation of such acts of kindness has a big impact on building a better world. Their website is:

www.kindness.org

They have worked in partnership with Melissa Burmester and Jaclyn Lindsey to publish a book called *Be Kind—A Year of Kindness, One Week at a Time.* The book encourages people to take an act of kindness every week for a year, benefitting others, (and therefore themselves), while deepening connections in their communities. In the book, for each of the 52 weeks, there's an inspirational story, some relevant and thought—provoking statistics and suggestions for acts of kindness.

Another organisation dedicated to promoting the concept of *random acts of kindness* is the Random Acts of Kindness Foundation:

randomactsofkindness.org

They've designed exercises and challenges to help make kindness the norm at home and in our wider life. For example, in one of their challenges, each act of kindness is worth one, two or three *hearts* based on how challenging they are. *One-heart* activities are quick and easy, *two-heart* activities are more involved and *three-heart* activities are challenging and will take more time.

A final example of the power of small acts of kindness is the UK charity based in Hertfordshire, called *Small Acts of Kindness*:

www.smallactsofkindness.co.uk

In 2015, Lynne Misner, who is the charity's founder, took her first steps to encourage people to make small acts of kindness to alleviate the loneliness and isolation which people were suffering locally, especially in the winter months. She created the concept of *Warm in Winter* bags, filled with essential keep warm items such as a blanket, warm clothes and hot drinks. Plus information packs which might help the recipients to break out of the cycle of cold and loneliness.

After sourcing these supplies, friends and volunteers helped her to pack the first 50 bags and with the help of local care organisations, she identified vulnerable members of the community who would be the first recipients.

The charity now regularly sources and distributes practical gifts that reduce the negative impact that feeling lonely and isolated can have on older people's physical and mental wellbeing.

Examples of their current *small acts of kindness* projects include:

Warm in Winter gift bags

Many older people struggle to keep warm when the weather turns cold. The charity's aim, each winter, is to source and distribute up to 10,000 Warm in Winter gift bags that will help older people keep warm in their homes.

Christmas gift bags

Many older people have no one to celebrate Christmas with. Each winter the charity give a bag full of hand-wrapped presents to 500 older people who are alone at Christmas.

Partnership with Violet's Gift

At Christmas 2020, the charity announced a new partnership with *Violet's Gift.* This Christmas charitable project was set up in 2015 to provide gift donations to people in care homes with no loved ones. With the help of volunteers, wrapping and delivering they made more than 1000 gifts available to 31 Hertfordshire care homes.

The charity has now been officially recognised for their achievements by various bodies in the following ways:

- British Citizen Award for Service to the Community
- Age UK Spirit of Age Awards
- Prime Minister's Point of Light Award.

All fabulous examples of the power of kindness and how they can significantly enhance people's happiness—both the person who receives as well as the person who initiates it.

Action taking 3: using our power as consumers

Finally, in this section on *Action*, it's also worth exploring how we can take action which helps to make the planet a better and happier place.

When we buy something, it will have come from somewhere, been grown or manufactured and will have been transported from somewhere to the shop where we buy it. People will have worked hard to get it to us, in good condition and on time and may be subject to certain (often poor) working conditions. In Stroud High Street, in the UK, there was until recently a shop called the *Art of Clay*, (run by an artist called Clay), which had a sign outside that quoted the fabulous words of Professor Anna Lappe, the American author and environmentalist:

> **"Every time you spend money, you are casting a vote for the kind of world you want."**

As consumers, the more we can become aware of and critically ask questions about our consumption, the easier it will be to make the invisible consequences of our consumption visible.

For example, if we know the fresh food produce we're buying is flown in from a country which still struggles to feed its own people, would we still want to buy it? If we know that the bargain clothing we want to buy is made by people in a country thousands of miles away who have to work for less than a dollar a day (i.e. less than 60p a day in UK currency)—would we still choose to buy it?

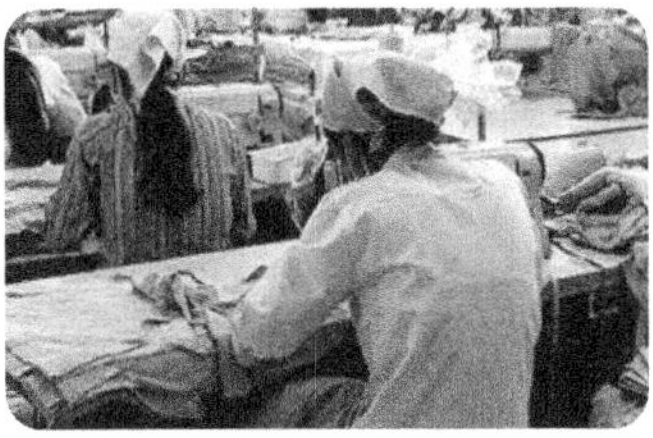

There's already evidence that one of the consequences of the pandemic may be a shift in some of our buying habits. According to Barclaycard, spending at local shops rose by almost 40% in April 2020. Of course, this behaviour may have been influenced by other factors such as long queues elsewhere, but a separate survey by the same card provider found that many people were planning to increase their spending at local shops, cafes and farmers' markets in the future.

Once upon a time, shoppers would glance at the price tag, perhaps the *made in* label or materials and ingredients and then decide whether to buy it. Nowadays, amid greater awareness about the environmental, social and geopolitical costs and impact of just about every product—from eggs, coffee, salmon, meat and motor cars—our shopping choices provide a great opportunity to develop the habit of *pausing before buying* and considering the ethical issues raised by the thing we are tempted to buy.

Workers' rights and safety, living wages, use of plastic, health and safety and environmental and social stewardship are some of the key considerations for us now as consumers.

Morgan Stanley Research recently surveyed 1,000 customers in the UK for their views on leading clothing retailers and found that, while ethical concerns don't dominate shopping habits—prices and quality still rank highest—they have gained prominence since 2010, particularly with younger consumers.

One welcome example of consumers developing the habit of choosing to buy food locally and having more certainty of, for example, where it came from is the increasing number of farmers' markets.

The success of farmers' markets in lots of towns and countries, is real evidence of a significant and growing shift in people's mindsets. In 2009, a report by the National Association of British Market Authorities (Nabma) suggested that 25% of the UK's local markets would close down by 2020. By 2013, however, its findings showed the farmers' market sector more than holding its own, with 65% of Nabma members reporting stallholder numbers up, 57% reporting higher footfall and 58% reporting profits either up or stable, year on year.

Farmers' markets provide many benefits to local people, businesses and their community, including reducing the carbon footprint of goods which otherwise might have to be transported even from country to country, encouraging more products to be produced ethically and not least adding to the vibrancy and happiness of communities.

In America, since 2008 there's been a dramatic 80% increase in the number of farmers' markets.

The first farmers' market in the UK was established in 1997 in Bath, with the support of Bath and North East Somerset Council. There are now at least 650 farmers' markets operating in the UK and with great success. One of the most successful is based in Stroud, Gloucestershire which has been awarded with the prestigious Farmers' Market of the Year award on many occasions.

The Stroud Famers' Market is strongly supported by Stroud District Council and Stroud Town Council. Both Councils also support the town's local community interest company called *Stroudco*, whose mission is to be a reliable not-for-profit online supplier of ethical local groceries for people living in or near Stroud.

Stroudco base all their activity around their *4 core values* which are:

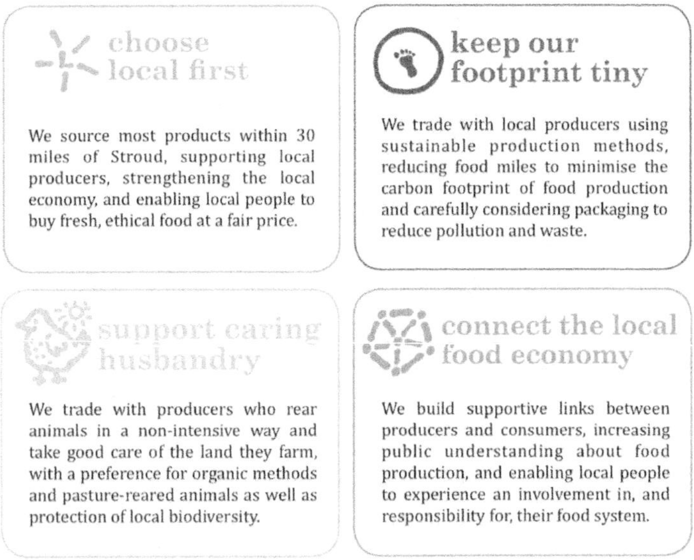

Stroudco's website is:

www.stroudco.org.uk

This is a wonderful example of the ripple effect, whereby one tiny change can create a significant ripple effect on the wider environment and an example of how we as individuals or as organisations can *turn tiny steps into giant strides.*

For example, when considering whether to use certain suppliers for online goods, *Stroudco* asks this series of questions, each of which strengthens the positive ripple effect of the purchases made:

- is the supplier local?
- are the goods produced with care for the environment?
- are any animals well looked after?
- is packaging kept to a minimum and ideally is it recyclable?
- is food organic, if possible?
- is energy used in the production of any goods used efficiently and ideally is it green energy where possible?
- are staff involved in the production of the goods well looked after?

As a result, producers who deal with *Stroudco* match and share their values of buying local produce where possible, keeping their environmental footprint tiny, caring husbandry of animals and connecting the local food economy.

Stroudco are an inspirational example of manifesting Anna Lappe's statement about *every time we spend money, we're casting a vote for the world we want to live in.*

Against all this background, there's growing evidence to suggest there's now beginning to be a significant shift in the buying habits of many people who are using their power as consumers to create the *win, win, win* habit of:

- good for us
- good for others
- good for the planet.

Our challenge as a society is to develop this kind of momentum more widely and make it the *new normal* way of consuming. There is also another question which we must answer as an individual and a society:

How can I seek my own happiness without creating unhappiness for others and the planet?

In our first book on happiness called *Finding Happiness After Covid-19*, we introduced the following 3 part model of happiness, which points to the need to seek happiness not just for ourselves and others, but also seek to build a new and happier life for the planet:

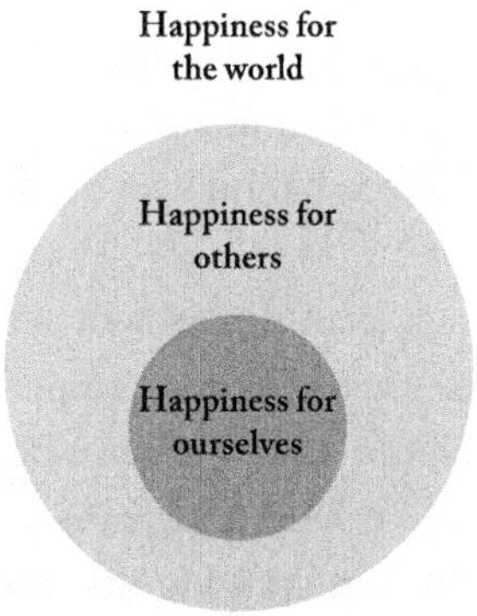

So, when it comes to taking action to increase happiness, we have plenty of options and potential starting points, including things that increase our own personal happiness, random acts of kindness to help others and finally using our power as consumers, through the choices we make as consumers to help make the world a happier place.

For how can we justify pursuing our own personal happiness if this damages others' happiness and the wellbeing of the planet, on which we all depend?

In Summary

In this chapter, we've looked at a number of ways that action taking can be made more habitual in our lives:

- the benefits of making random acts of kindness
- how making small changes, (repeatedly) can have massive medium and long term benefits for our happiness and others' happiness
- the way we can make a big difference to the happiness of the world by using our power as consumers as a vote for the kind of world we want to see.

We trust you now have some actions, some differences in how you habitually think, feel and act to take into your life. And to embed as new habits. In an earlier chapter, we used the metaphor of how the tiny acorn grows bit by bit into a great oak tree:

As a model of how most of us grow and develop, it's a powerful one . . . using the power of our brains to create habits in how we think, feel and act.

FINAL THOUGHTS

We hope that by the time you've reached this page, you already have some actual or possible starting points for actions. At the end of each chapter, you'll have noticed that we've invited you to pause, have a coffee break and maybe jot down some thoughts or questions. You may even have taken up the suggestion of starting *a journal* as a place to keep and develop your thoughts, ideas and actions. If you've done this, you'll already have a good sense of your next steps.

Just to recap though, in this book, we've explored the 7 components of happiness, leaving you with some tips about how to move forward on them.

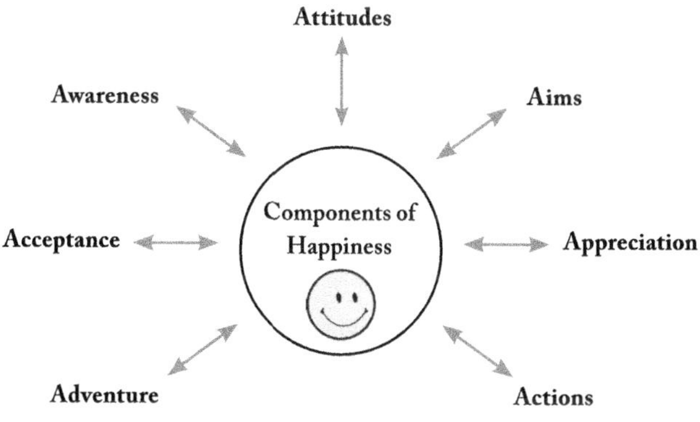

We've also given pride of place in the book to the *Action for Happiness* movement and the resources and help it provides, as we all seek to develop happiness and wellbeing.

It's possible though that you may still be wondering *where's the best place to begin?*

Our suggestion would be to follow this process:

- *sleep on* this question overnight
- on the next day, revisit chapter 7 on *Aims* and do (or redo) the exercise at the start of this chapter, which helps you to identify the factors that are most important in your life right now. (This in effect gives you your compass for the journey)
- decide to take a tiny action today which moves you in the right direction, focussing on one or more of the factors that you've identified as being of most importance to you in life
- repeat that action or take a similar action until you've developed a new habit.

One thing's for sure: if you change nothing, nothing will change, for as Henry Ford said:

> **"If you always do what you've always done, you'll always get what you've always got."**

We live in a society which encourages us through advertising and social media to believe that we can somehow *buy* happiness—a new kitchen, a new house, a holiday or a new pet, but we all know, deep down, that such thinking has its limits.

> **If you want happiness for an hour, take a nap.**
> **If you want happiness for a day, go fishing.**
> **If you want happiness for a year, inherit a fortune.**
> **If you want happiness for a lifetime, help somebody.**
>
> **—Chinese proverb**

We also live in a society which tends to assume that *doing something* means taking action in the external world, such as for example, sending someone a gift in the post. Of course, doing things of this sort can be wonderful, but equally, *doing something* for our happiness more often than not involves a subtle change inside our heads, in the way we think, what we notice and pay attention to and listening to the quality of our self talk and changing it, if appropriate.

The following quotation goes to the very heart of how to achieve happiness:

> **"A butterfly, which when pursued, seems always just beyond your grasp; but if you sit down quietly, may alight upon you."**

Although often attributed to the American novelist Nathaniel Hawthorne, these words first appeared in 1848 in the *Daily Crescent*, a New Orleans newspaper. There are several versions of this quote, but they all have the same message about the essence of happiness—so much of it depends on how we manage our own personal inner reality—our mindset, our thoughts and our feelings.

And when these are in the right place, the right actions will take place, in ourselves, in others and in the world.

Good luck in all you do . . . and may good luck be a lovely new habit, bringing you lots of happiness . . .

May your repeated tiny steps become habits and turn into giant strides . . .

"One tiny step at a time. . . .
Turning tiny steps into giant strides."

So, now, over to you, to decide and commit to specific changes.

If you need any further support or help, you can contact Peter at info@peverelpress.com.

REFERENCES

Action for Happiness movement, www.actionforhappiness.org

Briggs K and Myers I, *Gifts Differing*, Consulting Psychologists Press, 1980

Breus M, *The Power of When*, Vermillion, 2016

Burton D, *The Fundamental Goal Concept*, University of Idaho, 1983

Burmester M and Lindsay J, *Be Kind—a Year of Kindness, One Week at a Time*, Murdoch, 2020

Clear J, *Atomic Habits*, Penguin Random House, 2018

Covey S, *The 7 Habits of Highly Effective People*, Franklin Covey, 2015

Duhigg C, *The Power of Habit: Why We Do What We Do and How to Change*, Random House, 2012

Dweck C, *Mindset: Changing The Way You Think to Fulfil Your Potential*, Ballantine Books, 2017

Emmons R, *Counting Blessings vs Burdens*, Journal of Personality and Social Psychology, 2003

Feldman Barrett L, *How Emotions are Made*, Pan Books, 2017

Frankl, Viktor, *Man's Search for Meaning*, Penguin Random House, 1992

Gardner H, *Frames of Mind*, Fontana Press, 1983

Korzybski A, *Science and Sanity*, The International Non-Aristotelian Library Publishing company, 4th edition, 1933

Lyubomirsky S, *The How of Happiness*, Piatkus Press, 2007

McCraty R, *The Impact of New Emotional Self Management*, US National Library of Medicine, 1998

MacLean P, *The Triune Brain in Evolution*, Plenum Press, 1990

Maddocks J and Hughes D, *The Impact of Emotional Intelligence in the Workplace*, PSI, 2019

Peters, S, *The Chimp Paradox,* Vermilion, 2011

Porter E H, *Pollyanna,* Digireads Publishing, 1913

Post S and Neimark J, *Why Good Things Happen to Good People,* Broadway Books, 2007

Rohnke K, *Funn 'n' Games*, Kendal Hunt Publishing, 2004

Seligman M, *Authentic Happiness,* Free Press New York, 2002

Williams M Prof, www.psych.ox.ac.uk

Sumner, R. C., Hughes S. & Crone, D.M, Engage with your community with fresh eyes: Preliminary evaluation of mindful photography as an intervention to support wellbeing. University of Gloucestershire, U.K, 2019

ACKNOWLEDGEMENTS

We are deeply grateful to the following people for their wisdom, creativity, support and encouragement which have helped up create and publish this book:

John Seymour at JSNLP and JSA from 2002 to 2014
David Sales at First Ascent Group, www.firstascentgroup.com
Steve Bentley at First Ascent Group, www.firstascentgroup.com
Linh Thoi at www.lttebooks.com
Ken Dawson, Creative Covers at www.ccovers.co.uk
Martin and Val Adamson at www.martinadamson.co.uk
Jason Conway at www.cre8urbrand.co.uk
Beth Winbow, Stroudco at www.stroudco.org.uk
Ruth Davey, Look Again at www.look-again.org
Frances Kaufman and Lynne Misner at www.smallactsofkindness.co.uk

ALSO BY PAM & PETER KEEVIL

Published in 2020, this book brings together a toolkit of tips and techniques, some of which go back hundreds of years and some of which are based on recent neuroscience, all aimed at giving up options and strategies for happiness, especially in the light of the Covid-19 pandemic. It seeks to help us all to create *a new and better normal.*

This book can be obtained from Amazon and Kindle at:

www.amazon.co.uk/Peter-and-Pam-Keevil/e/
B08TCHGJQN

ABOUT THE AUTHORS

PAM KEEVIL

Dr Pam Keevil spent many years as a teacher, headteacher and trainer in both leadership development and personal development.

She completed a doctorate at the University of Gloucestershire on the personal development of school leaders in 2014. An MA in Creative and Critical Writing followed in 2016 and her novel *Virgin at Fifty,* a poignant and funny feelgood novel about starting over, was published by Black Pear in 2018.

For more information visit www.pamkeevil.com.

In 2020, she co-authored, with Peter, a book called *Finding Happiness after Covid 19*:

PETER KEEVIL

In the last 10 years, Peter Keevil has worked extensively with leaders of lots of organisations in the UK and elsewhere, helping them and their organisations to be the best they can be. Before that, he worked in organisational development in the Higher Education Funding Council for England in Bristol.

He's a qualified coach, NLP master practitioner and a qualified and experienced user of the various tools described in this book. He has a passion for everything that's explored in this book. He'd be delighted to hear from you and can be contacted at info@peverelpress.com.

We hope you've enjoyed this book and found it useful.

If you'd would like to be kept up to date with our Newsletters and other publications, you can sign up for these at www.peverelpress.com.

Finally, if you feel motivated, we would invite you to leave a review of your thoughts on this book on Amazon.

Thank you.

And don't forget, we're always happy to hear from you, using the contact details we provided earlier on.

And happy journeying . . .

Printed in Great Britain
by Amazon

35326311R00091